My Circus,

My Monkeys

Reflections on an Interesting Life

William L. Garner

Edited by Randy Tatano

This book is entirely a work of fiction. All names, characters, places, and incidents are either products of the author's imagination or are used fictitiously. Any resemblance to actual events or locals or persons, living or dead, is entirely coincidental.

Copyright © 2020 William L. Garner, Jr.

All Rights reserved, including the right of reproduction in whole or in part in any form whatsoever. For information contact wlgarner@williamlgarner.com

ISBN 978-09998916-2-9

To my wife, Landi , and the replacement units, Jiffener,
George, and the Catfish,
my sister Jackie, and my brother Matt,
Nana and Daddydoc, and my grandson,
Chaos Raby

Table of Contents

Introductions 1
Life Lessons 5
   Beware the Hookers 7
   The Gin 13
   How to Clean Carpet 15
   The Last Swim Meet 21
   Perhaps I Blew the Interview 27
   Volleyball 29
   37 West 65 35
   Surprise! 39
   Baseball 43
   Tips for Frying a Turkey 47
   Life is Better at the Sea 51
   A Wedding Toast 55
Family Matters 57
   Starry, Starry Night 59
   A Long Way from the Rice Fields 61
   The Bolivian Two Step 65
   The Journey to Boston 69
   The Good Stuff 73
   Ashley's Wedding 75
   Fang Skull 85
   Technical Support 87
   May 17th, 1929 93
   Memories of Christmas Past 95
   The Great Quail Hunt 99
   An Afternoon Movie 101
   Blessings 105
   The Gift 113
Friends 117
   In Memory of a Friend 119
   Abbie's Irish Rose 121
   A Dog's Life 125
   Old Friends and Memories 129
   First Love 133

- Duck Hunting 137
- The First Barbeque 141
- Brisket 147

Randoms 153
- The Old Man at White Horse Tavern 155
- Just Another Dad …for a day 161
- The Saucon Valley Country Club 163
- The Van 169
- It was an Ordinary Road Trip 173
- Superbowl 177
- The Worst Place Ever 183
- A Good Kid 193
- Dining with History 195
- Attacked by a Mad Dog 197

Introductions

In 1975 I was graduated from Jonesboro High School. I thought I would blow through college, go to law school, become a famous attorney like F. Lee Bailey, get into politics and become an American Winston Churchill.

Well, that didn't happen.

I selected my first college by virtue of it's proximity to my duck hunting fields. I was promptly kicked out of that school, and enjoyed a brief and aborted naval career. After serving a year of exile at a junior college, I entered the University of Mississippi. Despite my best efforts, my time at Ole Miss was marred both by graduation and a brief stint in Law School

In the nearly 40 years since that time, I have had a wonderful life. My family and life has been filled with innumerable encounters of meaning, glimpses of a reality that often leaves me wondering how I could have been so blessed. Some years ago, I began writing a blog in association with my competition barbecue team (The Memphis Barbecue Company – not to be confused with the Memphis Barbecue Company in Memphis which is a real barbecue restaurant). After publishing my first novel, *Me, Boo and the Goob: A Southern Adventure*, I continued my blogging in my own blog. Some of my blog entries are a mixture of truth, fiction, exaggerations and outright lies, but they present a reflection of the reality of a wonderful lifetime. While it can be said that not all of this stuff is completely true, it can not be said that any of it's spirit is false.

At the suggestion of several readers, I have compiled my blog entries into a single volume. I hope they provoke in you thoughts and memories, smiles and laughter, and the occasional tear. In working on this volume, I have again been reminded of what a wonderful family I have, what an incredible life I have lived, and what amazing friends I have.

Life has truly been good to me so far.

Life Lessons

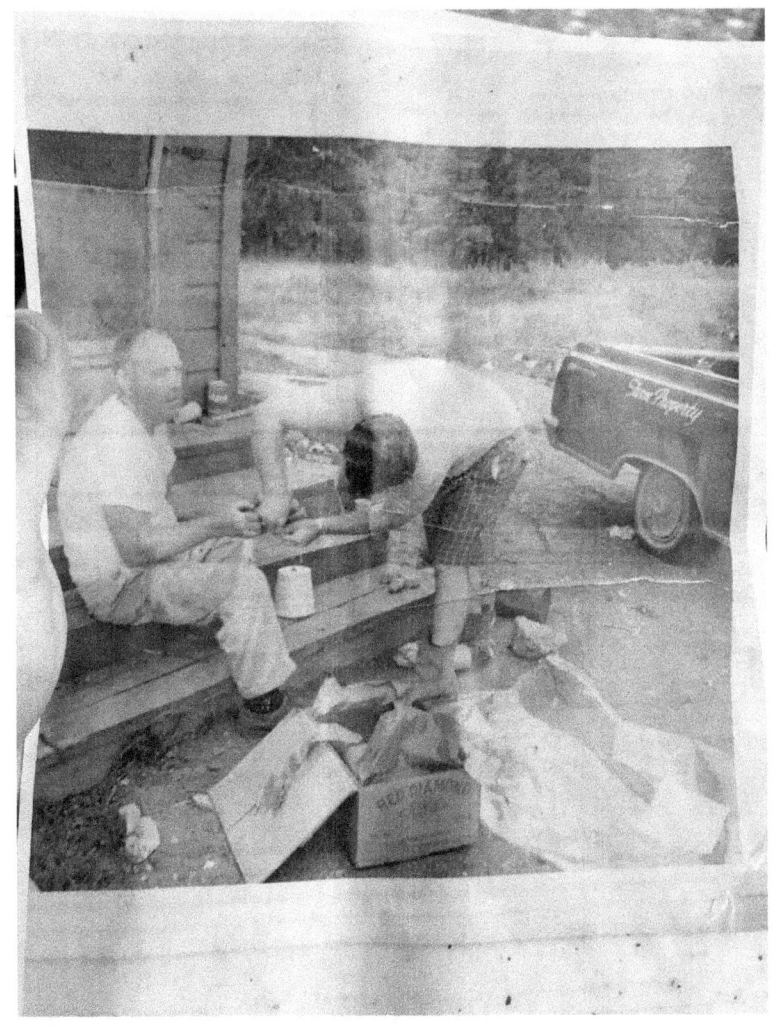

Beware the Hookers

I was excited about going to a casino, especially one in the Bahamas. I had never been to a casino anywhere, and what I knew about them I had learned from watching James Bond movies. I was excited at the prospect of playing roulette and baccarat surrounded by beautiful women. I was going to have a martini, shaken not stirred.

The day finally arrived, and I flew to Paradise Island. I was there for a meeting and although I spent the long first day in meeting after meeting, I paid little attention to the substance. My mind was already mingling in the crowd of international gamblers and spies awaiting me in the casino some fifteen floors below.

Finally, the meetings ended, and we all dispersed to our rooms. Some of the guys had brought their wives, but I was single so I was alone. I showered, shaved and carefully put on my tuxedo. I thought for a few minutes how lucky I was that my sister had mentioned to me there was a casino on Paradise Island, and asked if I had a tux. Of course I didn't have one, so the tux I was putting on was a loaner from her husband. It was just a little large, but it was OK.

Before leaving my room, I paused at the large mirror. I looked pretty damn impressive in my black tuxedo. My shirt was crisply pressed, the bow tie was striking. It was February, so I was pale as a sheet, but I looked sharp. I felt fresh after my shower, and as I looked at myself in the mirror, it showed. I sniffed the air and I could smell the Old Spice aftershave I had liberally applied. My hair was neatly combed, and I had put my cigarettes in a shiny, silver cigarette case. My lighter, freshly filled and sporting a new flint, was a Zippo. My watch was a Timex, and my tux, even if a little large, was absolutely perfect. I was ready.

It was early evening when I took the elevator down. I followed the signs in the hall to the lobby and then to the casino. I paused before entering to savor the moment. This was going to be fun. I could smell cigarettes before I went in, and hear the sounds of the one-armed bandits. I imagined the elegant crowd of international gamblers I was about to join. I took a deep breath and I pulled out my lighter. I confidently flipped my Zippo open, lit a cigarette and discretely checked out my debonair pose in the large mirror on the wall. I was Bond, James Bond. I walked into the brightly lit room like I owned the place. Through the haze of blue smoke, and the jarring sound of slots spinning and paying, I surveyed the scene.

The room was huge, covered with a thick carpet and sporting a very high, ornate ceiling. Slot machines with their flashing lights and ringing bells were everywhere. There was a crowd at some of the poker tables, but most were empty. The craps tables were loud and wild. It was kind of cold in the casino, and it smelled of stale smoke and nervous sweat. There was a low rumble from the conversations going on, and everyone was in Bermuda shorts and halter tops.

Bermuda shorts… and halter tops.

Everyone, that is, except me.

An older lady in a neon jogging suit approached me with a tray of poker chips. "Hold these, sonny," she rasped through her cigarette and she waddled into the ladies' room. I stood there taking in the scene, holding the tray of chips. The only people in tuxedos were the people who worked at the casino. Everyone else was in very casual attire. I realized I'd been had. After returning the chips to the bathroom lady, I went to the bar, removed my jacket, and sat down dejectedly. The bartender came over quickly, and thinking I was an employee of the casino, urgently said, "You know you can't sit here."

"I don't work here," I replied. "I'm just stupid." After ordering a drink, I told him the whole sordid story. From how I found out there was a casino on Paradise Island, having all my casino knowledge originate from James Bond movies, to how my sister had been so helpful with the tuxedo. I shared every detail. I explained how I got a haircut the day before I came to the island and that I had showered after my meeting ended today. I shaved and put my cigarettes in the silver case. I showed him my Zippo lighter and pointed out that it was freshly filled with fuel and had a new flint. The bartender and the strikingly beautiful, and obviously wealthy young lady across the bar found the story very funny.

I wasn't amused. I was a bit pissed until I realized that I was sitting at a bar in the casino on Paradise Island in the Bahamas, smelling good and wearing a tuxedo, telling a beautiful woman a funny story, and she was enjoying it. We began to chat, and she moved to the barstool beside me. For a long time we chatted, and I bought drinks.

After buying about three or four rounds of drinks, I was having a pretty good time. It occurred to me that this might be my lucky night. Her hair was auburn, her eyes were blue, and her accent was almost but not quite German. She was slender, but shapely and very fit, probably an athlete. I thought she might be a tennis pro, but I didn't ask. If she were some international tennis star, I didn't want her to ditch me thinking I was hitting on her because she was an international tennis star.

The woman, Chelsea, was as interesting as she was beautiful. She grew up in Europe, but now she spent the winters in the Caribbean and the summers on the Mediterranean. She had a degree in accounting, but found accounting boring. Yes, she did play tennis, and she spoke four languages, but said that I shouldn't be impressed. Many European languages are very similar, and being constantly exposed to several languages made it easy to learn them. We spoke for a long time. Finally, after furtively glancing around the bar as if to check that no one was watching, her eyes sparkled as she leaned over to me. My heartbeat quickened. She looked deeply into my eyes as she pulled me close so as to whisper something in my ear. I was excited. I may have been hyperventilating. I was hoping she was going to suggest we retire to her international tennis star deluxe hotel suite because I didn't think I had left my room in a presentable state. I wondered what kind of suite an international tennis star got at Paradise Island.

With a light German accent and in a soft, sultry and very sexy voice she gently whispered in my ear, "You realize I'm a working girl, don't you?"

There are moments in your life when you learn things. On this occasion, I learned that if you are a twenty-three-year-old goober from Arkansas, drenched in Old Spice and wearing a somewhat ill-fitting, borrowed tuxedo while sitting at the casino bar on Paradise Island buying drinks and talking to a woman who is clearly out of your league, understand that she's not there for the funny stories.

The Gin

The Gin was to Ole Miss what Rick's Cafe American was to Casablanca. It was more than a cross roads or a meeting place where libations flowed and inhibitions fell. It was a place where ideas were debated, and pretty girls were woo'd. A place where music rattled the walls of the old cotton gin just as hard as it rocked the souls of undergrads just discovering independence. The three tiers of seating offered tables providing great views of bands playing on the tiny stage. Tables overflowed with pitchers of beer, baskets of fried mushrooms and platters of fresh oysters. In the days before the smoking bans, the ceiling fans ensured a homogenized mix of cigarette smoke, perfume and cool, air conditioned air.

The Gin burned on March 6th, 2010. When I heard about the fire, even though I had not been there in nearly 20 years, it hit me hard. It was as if the Titanic had sunk or the Hindenburg had exploded. The Gin had burned. I didn't even realize it had closed. How the hell does that happen? A bar close in Oxford? Really?

On more than one occasion, I may have been over-served at The Gin. My friends and I frequently sat drinking beer, talking politics, philosophy and poetry while falling in and out of love in the dim light and swirling smoke of a rowdy Friday night at The Gin. Conversations erupting with everyone from Willie Morris to Mose Allison broadened our horizons more than anyone could have anticipated. The one universal truth that everyone can agree on some 40 years on is that we all knew that John Grisham was way too nice a guy to be a lawyer.

A night at The Gin was like a night at one of Gatsby's parties. It was loud, and there was laughter. There were beautiful people with wonderful futures hiding behind gleaming smiles while drowning their fears and insecurities in cheap bourbon and cold beer. The eclectic mix of cars in the parking lots described a crowd that included debutantes and dilettantes, jocks, accounting majors, law students and poets. No matter where you sat, or who you sat with, you were guaranteed a good night.

It wasn't a night at the Opera. It was a night at The Gin.

How to Clean Carpet

I usually start early, about 6:00 AM, on a day when my wife is traveling. This way I can vacuum the carpets, and shampoo them in one continuous operation without interruptions of conference calls and other realities of real work.

The first thing I do is check the vacuum cleaner. We have one of those bag-less wonders. It's really cool….unless the hose from the head of the thing to the container of the thing is clogged, which it always is. I don't understand this. How can a mechanical thing be so consistently fouled up. Anyway, quickly disassemble the vacuum, clear the entire path from snout to stern, and carefully reassemble the vacuum. Vacuum the entire room, being careful to dump the container because one false move and the damn thing is choked again. I am always impressed with the amount of stuff that comes out of a carpet.

Next, retrieve the carpet shampoo thing from the garage, and start trying to remember where the cleaning fluid might be. Examine the cleaner, and note it is quite dirty and clogged in places with junk from prior uses. A prudent man might say, "hmmm…..I probably ought to clean this so it doesn't fail while I am working with it."

So, I begin to disassemble the cleaner, noting how creatively and ingeniously it as been engineered. I take each part of the path from the carpet head to the water collection vessel and carefully clean it with hot soapy water. I reassemble the cleaner. It looks like new.

I let the dogs, Dixie and Maggie, out and give them raw-hide bones to chew on. This is so I can take the dog gate between the living room and kitchen down. The area right there at the gate is in serious need of cleaning. It's almost black.

As I survey our beautiful white carpet, I note with some sadness that it displays the evidence of a life with two large, dark dogs who run in a back yard of red clay. Some say the carpet is now a subtle shade of orange, others claim it's pink. I don't know. I'm color blind.

As I'm about to pour the cleaner fluid into the dispenser, it occurs to me that my old friend Oxyclean might be of use. Do you remember the commercials where the guy would shout "Billy Mays here" and proceeds demonstrate how Oxyclean would safely clean anything? I do.

I read the label, and then I put one full scoop of Oxyclean into the hottest water I had, and stirred. It looked just like the stuff in the bowl on the commercial. I poured all that into the fresh water container on my carpet cleaner, and topped it up with more hot water.

I began to clean. Forward I pushed the machnine as it dispensed detergent, Oxyclean and hot water, and back as it sucked it back up. My machine is pretty large. It holds about two and a half gallons of hot water. After about 15 minutes, I notice something odd. The machine does not appear to be picking up much water as I pull it back. I stop to check the machine. The dogs are barking now.

In seconds I notice a troubling fact. It has not been sucking water back up at all. I felt the carpet. It wasn't just damp, or wet. It was soaked with water, detergent and Oxyclean. I quickly took the machine apart again. There is an 'o-ring' the is cleverly hidden behind a lip of plastic that runs around the big piece of plastic that is on top of the vacuum head. With an old toothbrush, I clean the o-ring and reassemble the vacuum. Ever since I caught my little brother cleaning golf balls he got out of the Country Club pond with my toothbrush I have made it a practice to always keep an old toothbrush around.

I start it up, and it works for one pass. Now, when you pull the cleaner back toward you on the 'suck it up' pass, it makes a horrible noise. I stop again. One of the plastic plates that form the 'sucker' head has come loose. The dogs are barking like mad. I decide to take a minute to figure this out. I put the dog gate back up, and let the dogs back in. they are very excited about the new smells, and Maggie expresses this excitement by barfing up not only the raw hide bone she just ate, but also the contents of the last 5 or 6 meals she ate. Maggie clearly feels much better, and Dixie decides that this is indeed a tremendous bonanza.

With dogs back outside and barking loudly, I clean up an extraordinary amount of dog puke from our tile floor. I turn to go and put a big clump of dripping dog vomit in the garbage can. I stride with my right foot, and plant my slipper into a puddle of dog drool. Dixie had experienced a Pavlovian response to Maggie puking and had created a small but very slick and deadly puddle of drool. Dog drool is slicker than K-Y jelly. My right foot hit the puddle and took off at the speed of light for the other side of the room. My left knee gave way, and I tried to grab a kitchen chair on the way down to break the fall. To some degree, I was successful. I was not injured by the fall at all. I got up and viewed with some amazement the result of the fall.

Somehow, I managed to sling dripping dog vomit across both the kitchen and the living room in one graceful effort. Not only were there chunks of oozing slime on the counters in the kitchen, on the vent-a-hood, and yes, on top of the refrigerator, but it was also found on the couch, the china cabinet, the book case. I wasn't concerned about the kitchen. It's tile. The living room is carpet. White…well…either pink or orange…carpet….soaked carpet….covered with chunks of dog vomit.

It is now 9:30AM.

It's gotta be 5:00 somewhere, right?

The Last Swim Meet

In early August of 1965, I joined the Jonesboro YMCA swim team. I joined on a Friday, and the state swim meet was held the next day in Jonesboro. I won third place in freestyle and backstroke, and would have had second in butterfly, but I was disqualified. Before that morning, I had never heard of "butterfly" and the kid who explained the stroke to me before the race didn't tell me I had to touch the wall with both hands at the same time, so I was disqualified. I swam competitively for the next ten years until I discovered cigarettes, beer and women.

Several years ago, my daughters Jen and Jordan were on the swim team in New Jersey. At the final meet of the year, the last event was the "parents relay." My daughters, having grown up hearing of my swimming adventures, and seeing my trophies and medals, were particularly excited by this event. Of course they insured that I was recruited to be on the relay team. I wasn't overly concerned about it because the other parents recruited for the relay team were about ten years younger than me and looked to be in pretty decent shape. We would be competing with the parents of the other team. I wasn't going to really sprint or anything.

In those days I still smoked, so naturally I watched the swim meet and cheered our team on while having cigarettes and beer in the bar/patio area of the swim club that hosted the meet. The teams were well-matched. It was a close meet. Though our relay would not officially be included in the point tally, in the end it would take a "win" by our relay team to produce a team victory in the "unofficial" tally.

Our relay team gathered behind the starting blocks. I stubbed out my last cigarette and handed my beer to one of the timers. I climbed up on the starting blocks which were higher than I remembered. I stood there... all five-foot-eleven, two hundred and twenty-six pounds of potbellied, hypertensive me. I was sporting a two-or-three-year-old knee length baggy bathing suit that still had a little sand in it from the last visit to the Jersey Shore.

I looked down the blocks at the other two relay teams preparing for the race. Their leadoff men were tall... much taller than me, and lean. They wore Speedos, had bathing caps with their team logo, and goggles. They were stretching and shaking down. What the hell? These guys really looked like swimmers! They weren't fat. They looked like early middle-aged competition swimmers. They were skinny and had long arms and legs. Compared to them, my whole team looked like fat Elvis and the Jordanaires wearing baggy swimming suits and having a bad hair day. Clearly we drank, smoked and wheezed every day while these guys obviously were running or swimming. They wore Speedos and caps and goggles while we wore faded swimming suits and needed bifocals.

"Oh damn," I thought to myself. "This is going to be ugly." I looked at the crowd, and saw my daughters waving and smiling at me. Looking at me on the blocks beside the tall, skinny guys in Speedos, my daughters saw "invincible dad." Everyone else saw a fat middle-aged man in a baggy bathing suit about to drown himself in a race against real athletes.

Oh, damn.

I looked back down the blocks and began to construct a plan to make this as respectable as possible. I knew I needed to be the first one off the blocks because that might be my only advantage. I've always had a quick start, and knew I'd really need it this time. Each leg of the relay was twenty-five yards, so if I beat them out of the blocks, maybe it would take them a bit to catch me, and I could make this respectable.

I tried to shake down a little but the only thing that moved very much was my belly, and I'm sure that wasn't very attractive. I began to hyperventilate. I figured if I could go the whole twenty-five yards without taking a breath, it might save me a stroke or two. I continued to hyperventilate to get as much oxygen in my blood as possible.

The starter was ready, and called out, "Swimmers, take you mark!" I bent down into a starting posture that probably hasn't been seen in competition for twenty years. It was a little awkward. Swimming starts aren't normally done by a person sporting a pot belly. The starter's pistol sounded. In the corner of my eye, I saw that I had them off the blocks. I hit the water, and sprinted. It was only twenty-five yards but when you haven't sprinted in twenty years, that's a marathon. My arms were burning and getting tight after only six or eight strokes, and my lungs screamed for air. I wished I hadn't smoked that last cigarette. I could feel the muscles in my chest getting tight, the muscles under my arms start to cramp, and then with one final thrust of my arms, it was over. My right arm stretched out and tagged the wall. The next swimmer on our team flew over me and began sprinting his twenty-five yards.

I was wheezing, coughing and exhausted. My heart rate must have been two hundred beats per minute. Gasping for breath, I looked up at my teammate for help getting out of the pool, but he was looking at the other team. I turned and looked, thinking that we must have been smoked really badly.

Our second swimmer, who wasn't very fast, was nearing the halfway point of the pool, and the leadoff swimmers of the other two teams were just now reaching the end of the pool. I hadn't been smoked. I hadn't been humiliated in front of my kids. I had won. I smoked the tall lanky guys in Speedos, caps and goggles. I beat both of them by more than half the length of the pool.

With my chest pains beginning to subside, one of the other parents helped me out of the pool, and told me that my 'split' was a 12.3. "I swam twenty-five yards in 12.3 seconds?" I wheezed as I looked around for my beer. I turned back to the race. Our third swimmer was in the water, and we were still holding a half-length lead. I looked down the lanes at the other teams, with their Speedos, caps and goggles. Our fourth and final swimmer hit the water, and churned his way through the final twenty-five yards to victory.

Still standing poolside, wheezing and coughing, I reflected on the moment. From that first meet in August of 1965 in the Jonesboro YMCA pool, until this one, last race at a club pool in New Jersey, there was never a sweeter victory than this. I waved at my kids, swigged my beer, and looked for my smokes.

That was my last swim meet.

Perhaps I Blew the Interview

Along with everyone who isn't a professional pit boss, I find it necessary to have gainful employment for the sustenance of our family. Several years ago I was Vice President of Technology for an interesting company with unique leadership. Our CEO "bet" our "investors" that "he" could deploy not one, but two new data centers in 45 days or less and spend less than $2.5 million doing it. FYI, it can be done, but only if you actually order the equipment. Unfortunately, someone in finance missed that memo. Interestingly enough, one truth had become tragically apparent to me. You cannot build a first-class data center utilizing second class equipment with a third world mentality.

Anyway, in contemplating how I came to that particular point in my career, I was reflecting on some of the more interesting jobs and interviews I have had. One interview some years ago consisted of a non-technical and somewhat condescending recent grad of Brown reading technical questions to me, and then faithfully recording my answers verbatim on paper. Apparently, us techies can't be trusted to neither read nor write.

The questions were mostly useless "Unix Trivia" type questions with a smattering of real systems administration questions. The answer to one of the trivia questions consisted of a fairly complex command with several modifying arguments, so I told the young lady what command would be used, and what you would want it to do. She replied that she needed the exact command syntax. I told her that I didn't know the exact syntax. That if I were actually doing this, I'd look at the manual page because the arguments necessary to accomplish the task vary from one version of Unix to another.

With disdain virtually dripping from her voice, she sighed heavily and asked, "Don't you want to guess?"

In my senior systems administrator voice, I informed her, "Only idiots guess."

Somewhat peeved, she snarled, "Is THAT what you want me to write for your answer?"

"Do you need help spelling idiot?"

I think I blew the interview.

Volleyball

Nearly everyone I know has spent at least a few minutes watching the Olympics. My wife and I have watched more than our share of swimming. Last night we watched women's beach volleyball. It brought back memories of a picnic and a volleyball match in Memphis many years ago.

I was young, maybe twenty-eight or twenty-nine, and was a newly hired Manager of Data Processing at an Austrian Chemical company whose American operations were headquartered in Memphis. It was an exciting time. We were a $20 million a year business, and I was the head honcho of IT. My staff, split between Memphis and St. Joseph, Missouri, consisted of one full-time, and two part-time nerds. The company had sent me to New York for a couple of weeks to learn how the process manufacturing software worked. I was living large!

So, springtime comes around and we all work like hell. It becomes a 24/7 operation because spring is when the agricultural chemicals we made were used, thus, that is when we made the bulk of our product. We had a great year, and in August, our CEO Hans announced that the annual company picnic would be at some park whose name I have long forgotten. He also asked me if I would bring my grill and barbecue for the event. I was honored that he even knew I existed.

I arrived early the day of the event, started the fire, and began the prep work for the barbecue. I had to do a couple of batches of ribs and chicken in order to have enough for everyone. Other people arrived and set up for horseshoes, badminton and volleyball. More arrivals brought side dishes and beer. Hans, his lovely wife Maria and their two kids arrived. Hans held PhDs in both biology and chemistry. He was in his early forties while Maria was in her mid-thirties. Both were tall, slender and of athletic builds.

I have never been a fan of horseshoes. Badminton has never been my thing either, but volleyball… now volleyball was a hell of a fine game. We played it extensively when I was in the 7th grade. My jumping ability had really come in handy, and I loved the game. My 7th grade intramural team was the best in the school, and I fancied myself among the top players. I was looking forward to playing volleyball. All the while I managed the fire, I was thinking about volleyball. I remembered playing games so many years ago, and smashing the ball over the net. I remembered blocking shots, and setting up shots. I remembered launching limb snapping rockets at the other team and laughing as they cowered from the powerful shots that pummeled them.

Finally, the time to play was upon us. Everyone went over to where the volleyball net had been set up. Teams were chosen. Hans was on our team, and Maria was on the other. Each team took a few minutes to engage in minimal organizational discussions. In the end as starting positions were determined, I was to begin the game at left front. I was excited.

The other team had first serve. The ball came over the net, and was set up by the second line. Mike, starting the game at center, tipped the ball over the net, and it fell to the ground. We broke their serve. Our turn to serve.

We shifted positions one position to the right. I looked up and my heart sank. I was facing Maria, the tall and very beautiful wife of our CEO. She smiled at me. I melted. I have a competitive spirit, and I give one hundred percent in everything I play. I looked at Maria, an Austrian woman maybe five or six years older than me. She had blue eyes and blond hair that moved with the lightest breeze, along with a beautiful smile and a wonderful tan. She might have weighed one hundred and ten pounds. I knew right then that I wasn't going to blast the ball down this lady's throat. I knew that I wasn't going stuff her attempts to spike it. Hell, she probably didn't even know how to spike it. I felt horrible. I was all fired up and ready to play, and now this. I was simply going to have to go easy on this nice lady. Just then, Donna served the ball and in that instant my focus was back on the game. The second line fielded the serve, and set the ball up high for Maria. Instinct took over. I couldn't go easy. I had to play. I had to play hard. I moved swiftly into position to block Maria's shot. I was directly in front of her. She crouched a little in preparation to jump, and I did the same. Timing my jump just after her leap, I sprang high into the air, stretching my arms high to block her shot. I was going to shove this ball right back down her throat.

This was a mistake.

Maria leaped gracefully and amazingly high into the air almost like some sort of maniacal witch about to turn some poor slob into a newt. With no apparent effort, she soared high above me. I knew this wasn't a good sign. With a windmill motion that she performed with such speed that the air cracked like lightning, she wound up and struck the ball. She hit it with such force that tiny particles of ink vaporized as the ball shot toward me. I watched the ball in horror. It rocketed toward me as if it were a de-orbiting hunk of flaming space junk. There is no fear in the world like watching a searing volleyball of doom smoke the air as it closes in on your face.

I'm sure there was a sonic boom. The impact must have been on par with being hit by Mike Tyson. I don't remember being hit by the ball. I don't remember hitting the ground. I do remember the headache.

Maria had been a starter on the 1976 Austrian Women's National Volleyball team.

It would have been helpful to know that before the match.

37 West 65

Sometimes you run across something that really puts life in a new perspective. You pause for just a moment, and reflect on the blessings that you have been given.

Last week, Catfish and I had a wonderful weekend of diving. We dove in deep, dark, cold water, and he accomplished things that few kids his age attempt, much less accomplish. In training for these dives, and in acquiring the skills and knowledge to do so, he's achieving a maturity of thought at an early age. He's learning that anything can be accomplished with proper equipment and training. Anything.

On Wednesday of last week, his 8th grade class went on a three-day trip to Washington, DC. One of the places we visited was Arlington National Cemetery. It may not have occurred to anyone else, but it struck me that each of the heroes buried there was someone's son, someone's brother or sister, or someone's dad. Over six hundred acres of heartbreak. At the Tomb of the Unknowns, the click of the heels from the Honor Guard echoed across the plaza while three hundred 8th graders stood silently. The sun beat down on everyone, but the silence of so many lay very heavily on the moment. Again, the little voice in my mind whispered to me that this was someone's son, someone's brother, someone's father.

We then visited the Vietnam Memorial.   It lays like an open wound across a grassy field. At Panel 37 West, Line 65 the name Douglas D Estes appears.

On December 8, 1968, Doug was KIA: killed in action in Vietnam. He was only 18-years-old, and he was my cousin. I met him but once in the spring of 1968 at my grandparents' home. It was a hot day; he was smiling and laughing while horseback riding with his girlfriend. He had kind words for his little cousins. I remember thinking that he was so big, and so strong. He was a soldier. He knew how to shoot a machine gun. He got to fly in helicopters. He was there that one weekend, and then he was gone.

Only a parent can know the heartache of burying a child. As I looked at panel 37 West, Row 65, I remembered Aunt Dale's tears at Doug's funeral in Memphis. For a moment, I remembered Doug, smiling and laughing at my grandparents' home. I looked farther down the sidewalk in front of the wall, catching a glimpse of Catfish and his buddies looking somberly at the names etched in stone. A thought struck me like a bolt of lightning. I glanced up the sidewalk and saw only children coming down, looking at the wall. I turned back to the wall, and knew that each name was someone's child. I looked back toward Catfish and his buddies, but in that instant, they were gone.

I studied Doug's name on the wall again. It was there, but he was gone, and for just a second, I sensed the utter loss and profound sadness that covered Aunt Dale for the rest of her life. With a new insight, I moved up the sidewalk to find Catfish and his buddies.

Surprise!

Surprises come in all flavors. Some are good. Some are bad. I remember several years ago on my 40th birthday, Mom and Dad had sneaked into New Jersey for a visit. That was a good surprise. I enjoyed that a lot. Back in 2004, when we were in New Orleans to watch Jordan play soccer for Loyola, we had to cross the Mississippi River via the Huey P. Long Bridge. The Huey P. Long Bridge has two lanes with no apparent means of support, seemingly floating in mid-air on either side of train tracks which ran down the center of the bridge structure. It is about 1000 ft above the river and the guard rails that should prevent you from driving off the bridge are about twelve inches high. Hell, I've driven over curbs that were taller. When you are driving in a conversion van, or an SUV, you cannot see the guard rail. This was a damn bad surprise, a very bad surprise.

I closed one eye, repented of all my sins, and drove 15 miles an hour right down the center of the two lanes heading west. Traffic quickly backed up in my rear-view mirror, and the people right behind me were honking and flipping me the bird, but I didn't care. With everyone behind me leaning on their horns, flashing lights, and giving me the middle finger, I imagined that it must look like we were leading a parade across the bridge. We survived and I'll never, ever cross that bridge again.

Last week on our return trip from Florida, we were hopeful of avoiding an unpleasantness in terms of breakdowns, bridges or surprises. The Beast (pet name for the Ford Expedition) had performed flawlessly. On the trip down, we got almost twenty miles per gallon, and we figured out how to use the satellite radio. The DVD worked well, so Jordan and Catfish watched movies and studied. The only giant bridge encountered on the way down was skillfully avoided on the return route. The trip home was going alarmingly well. Too well.

On the first day coming home, we drove 540 miles, and got a room at a Marriott hotel in Knoxville, Tennessee. We were exhausted, hungry and thirsty. Landi, Catfish and Jordan went directly to the room with the bellhop, while I parked The Beast. When I walked into the lobby of the hotel, I noticed that there were about 200 tables set with beautiful white tablecloths, along with formal china in readiness for Easter brunch. I wearily stepped into the elevator thinking about how nice it would be in the morning if we could be out of here before all that got going. I punched '9' on the control panel, and the elevator began to rise. I turned around, and

HOLY SHIT YOU CAN SEE OUT OF THIS THING. IT'S ONE OF THOSE GLASS ELEVATORS!!! I was in a glass elevator rising like a rocket toward the 9th floor.

That was ugly surprise number one. As someone who has an increasingly profound respect for heights, I was stunned. I was in a glass elevator shooting up at an uncivilized rate heading toward the alpine region of this towering building. My fear turned to absolute panic as we neared the top and noticed that we were not slowing down. Clearly, we were going to hit the damn ceiling really hard. I grabbed hold of the hand rails tightly and braced for the collision. I wondered if the doors would open following the impact, or if the elevator would just break away from the elevator 'track' and plummet to the hard tile floor of the hotel lobby. I had visions of movie scenes where some poor bastard gets dropped from a really high place. Wile E. Coyote and Road Runner came to mind, but I had no illusions as to my ability to survive a fall like the coyote. I closed my eyes, and again, repented of my sins and some sins that I hadn't even done yet.

The collision never came, but ugly surprise number two did. The glass elevator flew through the ceiling and emerged into the blinding light of a dazzling sunset. My elevator was now on the outside wall of the damn hotel. It continued rocketing up the outside wall of the hotel like a rabid squirrel on a crack binge.

At this point, I was nearing incontinence. This had been a bad ride. I just wanted off the damn elevator. It was bad enough riding in an elevator inside the building, but this damn thing was now outside the building. Who the hell thought that was a good idea? If I survived this ride, I'd never ride another elevator. Finally, saints be praised and to the sound of trumpets, the doors of the elevator opened, and I exited the jaws of death. It took a minute to regain my composure and dignity.

I found the hotel room and went in. I must have looked a little shaken up, because Catfish and Jordan both thought my experience was exceedingly humorous.

Funny, my ass! I fixed a bourbon. No ice. No water. Just bourbon... a lot of bourbon. I was safe and in the room. I was out of danger.

Landi came out of the rest room and cheerfully said, "Okay, let's go down for supper."

I'm gonna need more bourbon.

Baseball

A few years ago, Catfish decided he wanted to play Little League Baseball. He's always been a "soccer kid" and had never really been interested in baseball. We go to see the Yankees about two or three times a year, but throwing the baseball in the front yard just doesn't happen. I never played baseball, so I didn't really encourage him to play. When he asked to join a Little League team, I thought, "What the hell... this will be fun."

That was an understatement.

Our team was a collection of about twelve or fourteen ten-year-old boys of various sizes, skill levels, and attention spans. We had one kid, a tall lanky pitcher, who threw smoke. He was probably the best pitcher in the league. No one got hits off this kid. We had another kid, a much shorter hyper-competitive pitcher, who threw almost as well, but would let the other team get into his head. One player, a big bear of a kid, showed up for practice about two weeks after we had begun training the team. He was a talkative boy and our head coach sent him to me. I was working with players in right field while the coach was hitting balls to us. We had a kid serving as a runner so that when the coach hit the ball, we had someone to "throw out." The big kid was explaining to me that he knew all about baseball.

The coach hit the first ball, a slow grounder, to the big kid. He trotted up to field the ball. The boy running the bases saw the big kid trotting to the ball, and kicked it into high gear, trying to make it to second base. He was really moving as he sprinted past first and toward second. It looked like it was going to be close. By this time, the big kid had the ball, and with a long and very athletic stride, he threw a rocket and nailed the runner in the back with the baseball about four strides short of second base. The runner went down.

It seems that the big kid actually knew a lot about dodge ball, and very little about baseball.

Catfish, on the other hand, understood baseball. It only took getting hit once or twice by a pitch for him to figure out that if he stepped backwards out of the batter's box, he would avoid getting hit. Unfortunately, when you are stepping backwards out of the batter's box, you don't hit the ball very often.

One Saturday, we were playing a pretty good team. Their pitcher threw hard and well. We just weren't getting any hits.

It was a scoreless game into the fourth inning. Catfish had come up to bat a couple of times, and on each occasion, with each pitch, he stepped back and out of the box.

Finally, it was Catfish's turn to bat again. Before he went up to bat, I told him, "Don't back out of the box." He looked at me like I had two heads, and said, "He's going to hit me with the ball." No, I assured him, he's not. "He hasn't hit anyone in the whole game." My words fell on deaf ears.

Catfish walked to the batter's box, and got set. The pitcher was ready. With a swirl of arms and legs that only a twelve-year-old boy can accomplish, a pitch came rocketing right down the middle of the plate, and Catfish stepped back.

Again, I called to him. "Don't step back!" He glared back at me, and got ready for the next pitch. Again, another strike emerged from the swirl of arms and legs, and again, Catfish stepped back. He looked over at me with that I know I'm in trouble look. I again told him to not step back.

He stepped back into the batter's box, and readied for the pitch. The tornado of arms and legs began again. Once more the ball came smoking out of the tangle, and sped toward home. This time, Catfish stood as still as a statue. He didn't step back. He didn't flinch.

The ball nailed him right smack dab on the kidney. It was a smoking fastball, and it got him solid. It didn't ricochet off and go to the back stop. It hit him solid on the kidney, made a dull thud sound and dropped at his feet.

He was kind of hunched over as he trotted to first base. As one of the coaches, I was allowed to go check on him. I trotted across the field and he glared at me. I could almost see smoke coming from his ears. He wasn't rubbing his back, but I knew it had to really hurt. I slowed my trot to a walk just a few steps short of first.

Before I could ask how he was, with a steely gaze he fixed his eyes on mine. As I neared first base, my ten-year-old son said "I told you he was going to hit me with the damn ball."

Catfish prefers soccer.

Tips for Frying a Turkey

A fried turkey is a wonderful thing. It is moist. It is flavorful, and it's not hard to do. There are some things that only experience can teach you, and toward this end, I have some advice to offer.

First, brine the bird. A brined bird is a juicy bird. Google Alton Brown's turkey brine and use it. It has some "interesting" ingredients. What the hell is candied ginger anyway? Don't worry about it. Get some and make the damn the brine just like he says, and sink the bird in it overnight.

Second, check you liquor situation. Though we generally start the day with a couple of rounds of bloody marys, I have found that a nice glass of wine is a wonderful thing to enjoy while the turkey is frying. We buy only the best of the box wines. I recommend the Merlot. Also, be sure you have ice and enough bourbon because after cooking this dinner, you'll be ready for a couple of strong cocktails.

Third, it takes a while to get the oil hot, so I go out three or four hours before I plan on cooking, heat the oil up to 340 degrees, then shut the heat off and let it cool. The main reason for this is to give me a good idea of how long it takes to get the oil hot. You want to cook the bird at 340 degrees, so if the oil has cooled to 200 degrees, and it took 90 minutes to go from 70 degrees to 340 degrees, all you have to do is find a 5th grader to figure out how long it will take to heat from 200 degrees back up to 340 degrees, and then most of us can figure out when we need to begin reheating the oil.

Fourth, it should go without saying that you should not fry the bird on a wooden deck, or indoors. The reason for this is simple. Since you've been drinking bloody marys all day, and you read the label of the turkey without your glasses, you will be operating under the assumption that you are cooking a twelve-pound turkey, not a fifteen-pound turkey. This is an important distinction because you filled the pot up with oil to the line for a ten-to-fourteen-pound turkey. That is a very important line. If you sink a fifteen-pound turkey into a pot filled to the ten-to-fourteen-pound line with boiling oil, the bird will displace enough oil so that when it breaks into a violent boil, some of the oil will splash over the side of the pot. Eventually, it will make its way to the open flame below. This, of course, ignites a fairly impressive fire, which interestingly enough, causes the oil to boil even more, violently splashing more oil out... and you can see where this is going.

Fifth, when extinguishing an oil and propane fire, the first thing you should do is turn off the propane at the tank. In theory, this will cause the fire beneath the pot of flaming oil to go out. You just have to trust me on this point because at this time half the concrete deck is on fire, and it is spreading into the yard. There appears to be a volcano spewing napalm on the deck and the propane flames are the smallest in the whole conflagration. You can't see them because of the big fire. It's important to get that little fire out first because if you don't, it may reignite the big fire a second time after you put it out.

Sixth, be very careful when using the fire extinguisher. I recommend setting your wine glass down so that you don't spill it when you pull the ring thing to use the extinguisher. Keep in mind that you'll want to aim the extinguisher at the base of the flames, and don't step in the oil.

Now you see why the bourbon is so important. I told you you'd want a cocktail.

Life is Better at the Sea

After being on Perdido Key for a week, enough time has passed for me to become acclimated to the sun, the sand, the sounds of the sea and plaintive calls of the sea birds. The water is warm here, and the people are nice. The sky is blue, and the breeze off the Gulf carries your troubles away. Perdido Key is indeed a paradise. As I look across the water of the Gulf, the light from the sun hurts my eyes. I think back to other visits to the Gulf, and to the wonderful times we've had here.

In early March, the water is warmer here than it has ever been on the Jersey shore. That particular thought drags me away. The Jersey shore is the Jersey shore. Some friends of ours found a corner of sanity down at the shore a few years ago. A place that was as lazy and laid back as the Gulf Coast. Landi and Darlene went bar-hopping on bicycles once. Our friends bought a condo on the mainland side of the bay, and it was feet off the water. You could sit on the front porch and watch the water much like we do here on Perdido Key.

We were visiting once, a couple of years ago down at their condo. It was a perfect day. The sky was as blue as it could possibly be. The sun was bright and warm. The beach, conveniently located maybe fifty feet from their condo, wasn't crowded or loud. At some time in the recent past, Joanie and Darlene had made a very wise investment in a Jimmy Buffet margarita maker. We didn't make margaritas, but we made a hell of a lot of daiquiris.

At some point, someone's cousin's niece showed up with a friend. The niece was in her early twenties, as was her friend. They both worked for a delivery company so they got a lot of exercise every day, and thanks to their string bikinis, it showed. I was ever so thankful for my sunglasses.

The nieces enjoyed the daiquiris and the beach. In all, there were about seven of us enjoying the beach, the sun and the water. The niece and friend applied suntan lotion to each other, which caused Catfish to stop breathing.

After some time in the sun, one of the nieces decided it was hot, and the two of them dashed down the pier and leaped off the end into the 'refreshing' water. We could hear them squeal, as could everyone else for a mile or two around. "The water must be really cold out there," I thought.

The nieces both swam quickly back to the beach. I watched them. They seemed to be racing. This is going to be interesting, I thought to myself. They neared the beach, and began to run through the water. I was frozen in time. It was almost like the scene from the movie 10. I felt dizzy, but thanks to my sunglasses, my gaze never broke from the two shapely young women in string bikinis racing toward me through the surf. I love the shore.

When at last they reached us, we learned that when they jumped off the end of the pier, they had actually jumped into a mass of jelly fish. They had been very badly and painfully stung all over their bodies. You could see the marks where they had been hit. Red welts were raising everywhere. The girls sprinted to the condo and began spraying each other with cold water from the garden hose, and rubbing the affected areas very vigorously. Catfish was transfixed.

When you become a Scuba Instructor, part of your training is a short course in how to deal with injuries common to an aquatic environment. Among these injuries are jelly fish stings which are very painful. When you are stung, a tiny pod of 'toxin' is stuck to your skin. First aid consists of dousing the area with a mild acid, or ammonia, and rinsing with warm salt water, never fresh water. Fresh water will cause the 'pods' to 'fire' again, depositing more painful toxin into the victim.

I went to my car, and got the large bottle of vinegar from my first aid kit. I approached the screaming girls. I told them I could help relieve the pain, but they would need to do exactly as I instructed them. Both of the girls eagerly agreed.

I explained that to ease the pain, I needed to slowly pour the vinegar on each of them, and that they should smear it around to ensure that all injured areas were heavily coated with vinegar. I took the top off of the vinegar, and began slowly pouring it on the chests and shoulders of the women. All sense of modesty was lost as they assisted each other in smearing the vinegar everywhere. EVERYWHERE. At this point, Catfish had not blinked in close to five minutes, and I'm pretty sure I hadn't taken a breath in close to eight minutes.

As the last of the vinegar was expended and the girls were much relieved from their pain, I finally breathed again. I looked at the small crowd that had gathered to watch the spectacle. A big, biker-looking guy smiled at me. He glanced at the girls, and looked back at me.

"Some people would pay good money to get to do that," he said, then he turned and walked away.

A Wedding Toast

Laugh loud, laugh long, and laugh hard.

Smile.

Have a short memory and a big heart.

Lift each other up, and help each other down.

Eat a hot dog, and drink Cabernet Sauvignon in the rain.

At the end of the day, be a hug and a smile.

Be a harbor, not a storm.

Be a rainbow, not a raindrop.

Live large, eat well, rest easy.

Wear bright colors, sing at the top of your lungs, and dance like there's no one watching.

Forgive quickly, forget quicker.

Walk together, hold hands, kiss often, and love madly.

Fall in love all over again every morning.

Life is short; put the wind at your back, and the sun in your face

Chase tomorrow forever.

Family Matters

Starry, Starry Night

On a starry night in the spring of 1954, a dashing young doctor met a beautiful young nurse on the Skyway at the Peabody Hotel in Memphis, and they danced. In November of 1954, they married, and through house fires, tornadoes, three children, many dogs and a multitude of adventures, they laughed and loved, and lived a very good life. Saturday nights always meant steak. In the late sixties, birthdays meant a trip to Shakey's Pizza. Saturday afternoons in the fall revolved around Archie and the Ole Miss Rebels.

Sadly, the dance ended far too soon in November of 2000, when the now aged doctor went to his reward. The nurse spent the next ten years shamelessly spoiling dogs and grandchildren. Miss Lady, a land shark masquerading as a poodle, frequently enjoyed breakfasts of scrambled eggs, sausage and the occasional finger. Sleepovers at Nana's often found six kids in matching pajamas in front of the television set watching The Sound of Music.

Saturday morning, two weeks ago, the nurse and the doctor danced again. We all will miss her, but she always loved to dance with her dashing young doctor.

A Long Way from the Rice Fields

When Jordan was just a baby, I used to look out over the rice fields from my perch high on Crowley's Ridge and pray that she would grow up knowing that there was a whole world out there full of challenge and excitement. I wanted her to know that Paris was the city of lights in Europe, but Beirut was its counterpart in the Middle East. I wanted her to know that while Memphis dry rub was the way to do ribs, the Carolinas really have pulled pork down right. I wanted her to sing the songs of Hank Jr., Elvis, the Boss, and Lynyrd Skynyrd with equal passion. It was important to me that she know the difference between Kentucky Bourbon and Tennessee Whiskey.

At thirteen, she transitioned from a tiny school in a tiny town in Arkansas to a pointy-headed private school in New Jersey. She didn't know a soul here except for Landi, Catfish, Buckwheat and me. She had never lived through a "Jersey winter" but she had survived many an Arkansas summer. She had never even seen a soccer game played when she went out for the soccer team at school. Four years later, the pointy-headed private school awarded her the Wigdon Cup recognizing her as the most athletic girl her senior year.

The first week of August marked her first year of college,

bringing good news and bad news. The good news was that she had made the soccer team at college. The bad news was that Katrina was coming in, and that New Orleans was evacuating. She wound up never playing college soccer, but she graduated with honors from Tulane, and got a full ride scholarship to UMass/Amherst for her Master's.

She has her Master's degree, and she'll be 24 years old in September. She has a job lined up in Indianapolis, and will move there next month. It's just now soaking in that Indianapolis will be "home" for her. It's not like the time in college, when she was gone, but "here" was still "home." Home will be "there" in Indianapolis. MapQuest claims it's eleven hours and thirty-five minutes away. That's a long way. To me, it's a lifetime.

I'd like to visit the spot on Crowley's Ridge where I used to stand and look out over the rice fields. This time of year you can see the farmers working the fields. From up on the ridge, it looks like nothing has changed in the last twenty-four years, but so much has changed. She has seen the lights of Paris and grandeur that was Rome. She has shopped the bustling, dusty markets of a North African town. She's stood on Times Square to welcome the New Year. She'll holler Hotty Toddy or Go Yankees with equal vigor. She can speak to you in English, French or Arabic. She's all grown up now, and I am so very proud, and, yes, she'll always be my little girl.

The Bolivian Two Step

Several years ago, I was shopping at Costco. As usual, I got steaks, bourbon, wine, and a mountain of other necessities. As with many big box stores, the downside of shopping at Costco is the checkout process. On weekends, the lines are invariably long and slow moving which is why I choose to go on Wednesdays right when they open the doors. I fly through Costco like a rocket. I'm usually finished collecting my goods in ten minutes, and standing at the checkout counter no later than twenty minutes after I first entered the store.

On this particular occasion, I was first at the checkout line. I handed the young man my Costco card. He was roughly my daughter's age. He scanned it, looked at it, and happily said, "Hi Mr. Garner, how's Jenn?"

Jenn, my first born, is a local legend. She is a graduate of a local private school, and in the year-and-a-half she attended the school, she had made quite an impact. Everyone knew Jenn Garner. She had that funny Australian accent. She won numerous sports awards, was named to the school Judiciary Council, was the starting goal keeper on the soccer team, and starting catcher on the softball team. Her grades were astounding.

At the time of this particular visit to Costco, though, she was a student at Mount Holyoke College. It was summer break, and she had gone to Bolivia to help mountain top peasants learn to do something useful. Unfortunately, those noble plans were on hold because at this moment she was languishing in a hospital in some tiny town in Bolivia having picked up a happy thing called "The Bolivian Two-Step," or, as we would call it, "typhoid fever." The "Two-Step" got her a helicopter ride from the mountain top to a Bolivian hospital for about a month's stay.

So I told her friend about her trip to Bolivia to help poor Bolivian peasants learn how to survive better on isolated mountain tops. I expressed to him how I had cautioned her about going places alone. When in pubs or cafes, I cautioned her, always sit near a door but not in front of a door; near a window but not in front of a window. Look at each patron, I explained to her, and try to figure out their "story." If something doesn't make sense, leave quickly but leave inconspicuously.

The young man just listened and hardly blinked. I explained about how she was very serious about international relations and studies, and that her Spanish was flawless.

Unfortunately, she had eaten something she probably shouldn't have, most likely a salad, because she picked up a nasty intestinal bug that really knocked her down. She's doing okay there in the hospital, I explained, but I could only speak to the nurse who spoke English because I speak no Spanish at all. Right now, I explained, we are just trying to get her healthy enough to come home.

The kid just blinked at me with eyes wide. "Relax, kid," I told him. "She'll be just fine once we get her home."

He finished ringing up my items, and looked at me again as I paid my bill. "Jennifer Garner is in a Bolivian hospital because she ate a bad salad and came down with The Bolivian Two-Step?" he asked.

"Yep," I said, "but she's getting better and will be home soon." Glancing at his name tag, I said, "I'll tell her you asked about her, Jeff."

He just blinked at me and I left.

I was driving home when it occurred to me that he was probably talking about the actress Jennifer Garner.

The Journey to Boston

In little more than 4 weeks, we will be visiting Jonesboro, my home town. As has been my habit since dad died, when in town, I will go out to the cemetery with some bourbon, and have a drink with dad. Mom is there now, as are Coachie and Miss Dot. This will be a tough visit. Dad's been gone for thirteen years, Mom for three, Miss Dot for eleven, and Coachie for two. I have to have a drink with each, and stop and visit with Dr. McKee too. Scott's mom and Frank are near Coachie and Miss Dot, so we share a drink too. Usually, when I visit, I am melancholy. I miss them all so very, very much, and I have to have a designated driver for the visit.

On this visit, I'm not going to be melancholy. I have good news to share.

On May 17th, 1986, in St. Bernard's hospital, a little girl was born. We named her Jennifer. She screamed bloody murder, and began a journey. None of us are born the person we will be. We are all the product of our mentors, our experiences, our decisions, and our determination. She left everything she knew in Wynn, Arkansas for Australia when she was a junior in high school. On her return from Australia, she moved to New Jersey. After spending half a year studying beer in

Australia, she dropped mid-year into a pointy-headed intellectual school in New Jersey, and took up soccer, a game she had never played before. She excelled. With each challenge she found, she found greater strength, and more resolve. Daddy Doc would have been so proud.

She was accepted into Mount Holyoke. It's a women's Ivy League school. Two generations from the cotton fields in Mississippi, this girl is Ivy. She's Ivy not because she's a legacy. She's not Ivy because of a big donation or ethnic advantage. She's Ivy because someone on the admissions committee said, "Holy shit, look at this kid."

So, as with every kid, there was an idealistic streak that had to be massaged some via a year teaching Spanish in an inner-city school in New Orleans. She left New Orleans still idealistic, just a more worldly and knowledgeable idealist. She began law school, on her own dime.

She went to law school at night, working as a cheese monger first, and later as paralegal by day. She played rugby on weekends, and tormented both her sister and her brother at every opportunity. Buckwheat loved her more than can be said, but that is also true for Dixie, Chaunti and especially for Tony Perez... and for most folks who have known her. Landi and I count ourselves as being lucky to know many of her friends, some dating back to high school. One, a doctor in the making, is like another daughter to us, and her father is one of the few people on this earth in whom I have absolute trust. She has just as good a taste in friends as she does in dogs.

Tomorrow, my journey to Boston will be a short one. South Plainfield to Boston isn't long or hard. It's four lane all the way. Though her journey began in the rice fields of Arkansas, it took her through Australia, Jamaica, Spain, and Bolivia. It was a journey of academic and self-discovery. She has triumphs that only the birds saw, and failures that only she perceived. She struggled and no one knew because she just kept on going. Success could not elude her.

Strength isn't succeeding when everyone cheers for you. Strength is when you prevail when no one knows you are struggling. She made everything look easy.

She gets her license to practice law in Massachusetts tomorrow.

The Good Stuff

All the grandchildren said the house was haunted, and they just may have been right. Fifty years of Christmas Eve quail dinners linger long in the kitchen. That just doesn't fade away very quick. On the patio where thousands of cocktails were consumed and countless steaks were cooked on a gas grill beneath the spreading branches of the old "acorn" tree, the ghost of Daddy Doc smiles back at me in a reflection off the French doors. In the den, the footstools were gone, and it's a sure thing that my brother still can't fly. In the tile, Mom's reflection glared at me, and I'm sure she's still pissed. Somehow, it was my fault that my brother couldn't fly. The memory of Miss Dot sitting in all her finery on the lounger in the den, sipping a cocktail, smiling and telling us all "one damn thing." Don't blink, you'll miss her. Yeah, that house was haunted.

On the last weekend, to the casual observer, the house appeared mostly empty. We, the kids, had removed furniture. As we went from room to room sorting out memories and wading through smiles and tears, it became clear to me that this house would never really be empty. Though Mom and Dad were gone and no longer lived there, and despite being emptied of its contents, this house would always be full of history. Just stepping through the door brings back floods of memories and emotions. Though the pictures have been taken down from the walls, the memories still float in the air like the whiff of a familiar perfume on the breeze.

In emptying the house, we closed a chapter. We each came away from our home with things to remind us of Mom and Dad. Mom will always smile back at me from her secretary. Though I have to call my sister for help with the recipe, I'll forever see Mom every time I use the corn bread stick mold. In looking at the swords, I'll remember her antique store. Dad will forever be sitting on the couch, cigarette and cocktail in hand, explaining things to me. He had a certain clarity of thought.

On this, the last weekend in the house, the memory of the old grump sat smiling on the couch.

I understand.

Ashley's Wedding

Just last month, my nephew married a wonderful young lady in an incredible ceremony in my hometown of Jonesboro, Arkansas. Despite a raging thunderstorm during the rehearsal dinner, the whole weekend went off like clockwork. It was incredible. On our flight back to New Jersey, I had time to think about the wedding, and about the impending wedding of my daughter. I anticipate all sorts of madness, as Jordan's wedding will be in New Orleans. A couple of years ago, one of my nieces had a wedding in New Orleans and it was a fantastic event. As the jet flew me home to Jersey, I looked down on the passing countryside, and slowly, another wedding came to mind.

Roughly ten years ago another niece, Ashley, held her wedding on a sweltering evening in mid-August. Everyone thinks they know hot. Everyone thinks they know humid. If you haven't spent an August in Jonesboro, Arkansas you know neither hot nor humid. In August, if the air moves at all, you feel more like a dog is panting on you than anything else. The warm and oh-so-humid dog breath breeze does more than make you uncomfortable. It makes you miserable because it usually is just enough breeze to bring airborne visitors from the rice fields south of town into Jonesboro. At the last puff of a breeze, mosquitoes the size of sparrows swarm like flying vampire biker gangs and immediately begin sucking blood, bone marrow and the very life force from those unfortunate enough to get caught in either darkness or shade. Home sweet home.

On the day of the wedding, my wife and I were supposed to make sure Mom was at the church on time. That was our mission. Get Mom, and get her to the church with time to spare because Momma's not happy when Momma has to hurry. Mom likes to take her time getting ready, and so Landi and I enjoyed a couple of cocktails while Mom finished getting ready. Landi was as beautiful as she has ever been with every hair in place, and perfect makeup. I was wearing my freshly pressed suit. I had my crisply starched white shirt with the French cuffs sporting my gold Ole Miss cuff links. My freshly cut hair was neatly combed. We were a sharp looking couple. Ten minutes before we were going to leave for the church, and a full twenty-five minutes before the wedding, the phone rang. It was my sister.

"You've got Aunt Dorthy?" she asked.

"No," I replied. "Am I supposed to?"

"Mother was supposed to get Aunt Dorthy from the nursing home," came the response.

"Shit... okay, no sweat. I'll take care of it," I assured her, and I hung up. I told Mom that we had to get Aunt Dorthy. After a brief discussion, it was decided that Mom would drive herself to the ceremony, and that Landi and I would go get Aunt Dorthy from the nursing home and take her to the wedding. We fixed fresh cocktails, and headed out. It was a ten-minute drive to the nursing home. On the way there I explained to Landi just how big a role Aunt Dorthy had played in our family for so many years. First, I explained that Aunt Dorthy wasn't really an aunt, but that's what Dad had always called her. She had worked for Mom, and later for my sister, for many years. She had a big part in raising all of my sister's kids. I hadn't seen Aunt Dorthy in some years. It crossed my mind as we sped through Jonesboro streets to the nursing home, that this might be a very fortuitous event because we'd get to spend some time with Aunt Dorthy. We pulled up in the parking lot of the nursing home and I walked quickly to get Aunt Dorthy. I had parked as close as I could to the door so she wouldn't have to walk far.

Having not seen Aunt Dorthy in several years, I was somewhat unprepared for what awaited me. Aunt Dorthy was dressed to the nines. Her hair was perfect, as was her makeup. Sitting there in her wheelchair, she was absolutely glowing…

In her wheel chair…

An orderly helped me wheel Aunt Dorthy out to the van. In the late afternoon heat of an August day in Arkansas, I was already starting to sweat. At the van, the orderly, citing some rule, decided he could help no more, and retreated into the nursing home. Landi and I set about getting Aunt Dorthy into the van. The van, I should mention, was fairly high. It had a running board that everyone stepped on to climb up into the van. It's not too difficult… unless you weigh four-hundred pounds, have two artificial knees and can't walk.

Aunt Dorthy slowly and painfully stood up. The wheelchair started to roll away, and I reached to grab it in case Aunt Dorthy needed to sit again, and as I stretched to grab it, I heard the tearing of fabric and felt the shoulder of my suit jacket… give… just… a… little. Damn. But I caught the chair, which was a good thing, because, with a pained groan, Aunt Dorthy sat back down. We locked the wheels of the wheel chair, and tried again. Slowly and wobbly, Aunt Dorthy stood. She was as tough as she was determined. With her right hand, she grasped the handle at the top of the sliding door of the van. She was making a superhuman effort and it was painful, but she was going to make it! Then, she started to fade. All sense of modesty lost, I shifted my position so that I could get my shoulder under her butt. I squatted down, and again, I heard the tearing of fabric, and felt a new looseness in my pants. I got my shoulder under her and lifted as hard as I could, but made little progress until I reached with my left hand to grab the frame of the captain's chair we were trying to get her in. Again, the sound of tearing fabric and a new freedom in my left shoulder told me I had torn that sleeve too, but not for nothing, Aunt Dorthy was now sitting peacefully in one of the captain's chairs in the back of the van.

I looked at Landi. Sweat was running down both her cheeks. Her running mascara gave her a little of an "Alice Cooper" look. Her beautiful dress was marked with sweat and wrinkled beyond belief. Her hair was… interesting. She smiled at me, and I smiled at her.

I was covered in sweat. I could feel my shirt sticking to my chest and I had torn the shoulder out of both of the arms of my suit, and split the seat of my pants, but in the rear-view mirror I could see Aunt Dorthy smiling in the back seat. I again looked at Landi, and she looked at me. We laughed a little and with the air conditioner going full blast, we headed to the wedding.

At the church, I stopped the van right at the handicapped entrance. I would pay the ticket if I got one, but I wanted Aunt Dorthy as close to the door as possible. Getting Aunt Dorthy out of the van was much less trouble than getting her in. With Aunt Dorthy safely in her wheelchair, Landi and I began trying to navigate to the church sanctuary. The signs directed us to an elevator. Emerging from the elevator, we saw a door marked "Sanctuary." Landi pulled the door open, and I pushed Aunt Dorthy through the door… into the sanctuary… the front of the sanctuary… behind the wedding party…during the ceremony.

As inconspicuously and quickly as possible, I wheeled Aunt Dorthy off the stage. With the ceremony in full swing, all eyes were on us as we slipped down the groaning ramp and into the handicapped space. I could feel my sister's gaze burning my skin. Landi sat down beside me. We were watched the rest of the ceremony and marshaled our strength.

After the ceremony, I asked Mom if she would ride to the reception with Landi in the van so I could put Aunt Dorthy in her Lincoln, and Mom was agreeable, so that's what we did. Hoping to beat the crowd, Aunt Dorthy and I went directly to my sister's house. I hoped that I'd be able to get a close parking place, but that plan didn't work out so well. Cars were backed up all the way down the driveway, so I drove past the house, and parked a couple of blocks away. I helped Aunt Dorthy out of the car into her wheelchair and began slowly pushing a four-hundred-pound lady back up the road in the smothering heat of a mid-August evening wearing the remnants of what once was a fine suit. The last leg of the journey was up the hill of the driveway. I had to really lean into it to get her up the hill because the leather soles of my shoes slipped easily on the polished concrete driveway. I was sweating like mad. My shirt was completely stuck to my back, and as the sweat ran down my face, and into my eyes, blinding me, I had to dodge a couple of cars that came flying down the drive, apparently driven by the "valet" parking guys. Valet parking?

Finally, we entered the reception. Aunt Dorthy was in her glory. She knew everyone there, and probably for the first time in her life, she held court. Everyone had to visit Aunt Dorthy! She knew everyone because she had watched them all grow up. While she was visiting with someone, she mentioned to me that she was a little hungry. Landi got her a fresh glass of wine, and I went into the dining room to fix her a plate from the buffet. My sister's dining room table is huge. It will comfortably seat thirty people.

On this massive table the caterer had done a magnificent job presenting an absolute abundance of wonderful food. It was incredible. As I surveyed the beautiful buffet, in the corner of my eye, I sensed, more than saw, someone bump a tall cabinet. The tall candle on the cabinet wobbled back and forth a couple of time, finally teetering just a smidgen too far. It fell coming to rest against the antique tapestry hanging on the wall. I shouted to the person beside the cabinet, but in the low rumble of the crowd he didn't hear me. I shouted louder, but no effect. Everyone was eyeballing the shrimp. I moved close, but the crowd, all waiting to get to the food, was slow to part. "That's on fire!" I said, as I pointed excitedly and pushed my way through a determined and hungry crowd. I was almost there, when with a muffled "whoomp" the tapestry burst into flames. It was a real fire, with flames nearly a foot tall.

The room went oddly quiet, and someone said, "Hey…that's on fire!" Now the crowd froze in place. Almost in unison they looked at the fire. I took this opportunity to drive my way through to the cabinet. I jumped up on top of the cabinet, and began pounding the flames with my bare hands, trying to knock the fire down. "Get me a towel!" I shouted to the nearest guy. He just looked at me. A very kind lady handed me a paper napkin.

"I need water!" I shouted. Someone keenly observed, "Dude! That's on fire."

Still, no one moved. No one put a plate down. The shrimp were going fast. I was pounding the fire with paper napkins and a plastic cup while sparks and smoke were filling the room. "I need something wet!!!" I shouted. Everyone split their attention between the food on the table and the fire on the wall, but no one paused from filling their plates. They were closing in on the roast beef. Finally, the chef ran out of the kitchen with a wet towel.

In just a few seconds the fire was out but not before leaving a huge hole burned in the tapestry, and an ominous black smudge on the wall, with those creepy smoke stains going up to the ceiling.

I climbed down off the cabinet and fixed Aunt Dorthy a plate all the while listening to the murmured comments about the fire. I took Aunt Dorthy's plate to her. She was still holding court and having the time of her life. Landi looked at me with horror…. and that "What the hell happened to you?" look in her eyes.

I went to the bar.

The bartender was facing away when I approached. He turned and looked at me. Startled, he recovered and slowly he took in the whole state of my disrepair.

My coat had both the shoulders torn out and the front pocket was ripped. My shirt tail was out and my white shirt was covered with black soot. My face was streaked with black soot and sweat. Sweat had run down my face drawing clear lines in the soot, and my shirt was stuck to me. My tie was badly burned and one eyebrow was completely gone. My hair was probably still smoking some. He sniffed the air, obviously taking in the aroma of burnt hair, sweat and wet plaster.

The bartender smiled, reached for the bourbon, and said, "You must be Uncle Bill. They warned me about you."

Fang Skull

At a height of about five feet, a kid has a different perspective on a lot of things. They know every dog in the neighborhood, and speak of the dog as if he were a friend. Property lines have little meaning. Nary a thought is given to cutting through back yards, side yards, and front yards on their way to the "woods" or a friend's house. They may borrow things, but they will never steal, and they will give you all they have for the asking. They haven't a clue about the value of a dollar, but they can tell you all about lucky rocks. At once, they treat their friends like dogs, and dogs like brothers. They are generous beyond good sense to friend and stranger alike, and loyal to the end even in the face of grievous punishment. I think they pick that up from the dogs. They ride bicycles and skateboards with the casual elegance of a soaring hawk, crash them like flaming train wrecks, and rise again bleeding, but smiling and laughing. They find more joy in a single jelly bean than we find in Christmas, and we try to teach these kids to be adults.

It seems to me, that we ought to consider becoming more like kids.

On Father's Day, my wife took my son to the world's greatest store (Spencer's) and bought me a gift I will never, ever forget. Having blown my knee out last September, and despite having it surgically repaired, it still hurts and I limp a little. If you limp, you ought to have a cool cane. A cane much cooler than any that Dr. House might possess. If you are a twelve-year-old boy, there is nothing better you can give your limping dad than a black cane topped with a skull with fangs.

If you are a limping dad, there is nothing better your son can give you than the look on his face when he sees you smile after opening a box containing the world's greatest cane.

It doesn't get any better than that.

Technical Support

Some years ago, my mother-in-law bought a new HP computer. She asked me to come down to Riverside and install her software on it, and move her documents and photos to it. I took my external drive and drove down, spending the afternoon installing the software and restoring the documents and photos. Everything worked, and she was thrilled.

The next day, about mid-afternoon, I get a panicked call from my mother-in-law. "IT'S GONE!" she screamed into the phone, "IT'S ALL GONE!"

"What's gone? What happened?", I asked urgently, fearing the worst.

"My programs…my photos….my documents! They're all gone!"

A 45 minute conversation finally revealed that earlier this afternoon, she had changed her password and then taken a nap. On waking up from her nap, she couldn't remember her password. Being unable to log in to her new computer, she called HP Technical Support, and some very helpful but mumbling and highly accented person somewhere in the Indian Subcontinent had walked her through the steps to reinitialize the operating system. The Tech support person never told her that she lose her newly installed software and data.

She was distraught.

I told her not to worry, I still had all her 'stuff' on my external drive, and I'd come put it back. She was very adamant about filing a 'complaint' with HP. I told her I would take care of it.

At the time, I was a consultant with HP. I was an 'Internal Resource'. I had access to internal HP processes, and I initiated a complaint using the proper HP procedure. I spoke with probably 30 individuals, each of whom would cheerfully explain, in a sing-song accent, with many interestingly pronounced words, that I 'simply didn't understand the way a technical support call functions'. Usually, it was at this point that I would remind them that I was an HP Technical specialist and I'd ask to speak with their boss. Finally, I reached someone who spoke English, and who could understand what I needed to communicate.

First, I explained that ordinary people have a hard time understanding technical support delivered by fast talking people with thick foreign accents. Not being judgmental, it's just a fact of life. Secondly, the tech support folks are delivering bad tech support. My mother-in-law should have been warned that her software and data would be lost if they reinitialized her system. Finally, I explained, HP will probably never sell another computer or printer in Riverside, New Jersey because my Mother-in-Law knew everyone in town, and being pissed, she just can't stop telling the story, and it get's 'better' every time she tells it. My contact assured me that he would make the 'powers' that be aware of this.

So, I called my mother-in-law, Elsa, to bring her up to date, to give her some closure. Have you ever had a stroke of inspiration? Just out of the blue, something leaps into your mind and it seems to be a really great idea? As she answered the phone, it happened to me.

"Hello", Elsa said as she answered the phone.

"My name is Sahiminash. I am with HP Technical support. I understand you have had a veddy minor problem that has not been resolved to your happy satisfaction?", I said in a heavily accented, sing-songy voice. And it began....

I coxed her to tell me the whole story again, nudging her on occasionally just to spin her up more and more. At every opportunity, I teased her just a bit to get her more and more angry. Finally, when I thought she was about to burst into flames, I interrupted her.

"May I put you on hold for a moment?", I asked in my thick accent.

"What?" came the startled reply.

"May I put you on hold?, I repeated in my unimaginable accent.

"Yes"

I held the phone away from my face just a tad, and in my wonderful accent, said just loud enough for her to hear…."Shoot him", pausing just a second, I slammed a book down on the counter creating a loud "Bang!"

"What did you say?", she asked.

"I had him shot. SHOOT HIM AGAIN, HE MOVED!", I replied. Once more, I slammed the book down and a loud 'bang' echoed through the room.

"WHAT?", she screamed into the phone.

"I had him shot. Shall I shoot another one. RAMADAMA! SHOOT ANOTHER!", I continued, and again the book slammed against the counter.

At this point my mother in law was losing her mind. It took some doing, but I finally calmed her down. She realized it was me, and somehow failing to see the humor in this, the cussing started.

It wasn't until weeks later that I learned that when this was going on, her preacher was there having coffee with her.

Let's just say Elsa never has appreciated the humor in this particular event.

May 17th, 1929

I heard him laugh just last week.

Catfish somehow failed to see a 6-foot umbrella in the yard, and destroyed both the umbrella and the hours-old lawn mower. I heard him laugh, and I could see him tilt his head back just a bit, and look toward the sky as he chuckled. It was a "I've been there, done that and bought the t-shirt" laugh. I haven't heard him laugh all that much in the last ten years, but he laughed at that. In his pale blue eyes, you could see memories of my many misadventures as a child... and in the echo of the chuckles, you could tell he was enjoying this.

I remember I once told him about something absurd that Catfish had done, he laughed a little and looked at me with smiling eyes, and said, "Has he burned the house down yet?"

I had to answer, "No, sir. No, he hasn't."

"Well, I'm one up on you then, aren't I?" he replied. And he threw his head back just a little, and laughed. I laughed, too.

When he laughed, he laughed with his whole body. Sometimes, it was just his eyes. Sometimes you could tell when he was laughing just by the way he was standing, even when he wasn't making a sound, and sometimes, it was just that look in his eyes.

As my daughters grow older, and accomplish greater and greater things, I hear from him at graduations. He doesn't laugh at graduations, but I still know he's there. He smiles really big. He had two gold teeth way back in his mouth, and when each of girls graduated from college, I'll bet you could see both of them.

As Catfish experiences the teenage years, I suspect I'll hear from him more often. I know he's looking forward to this. I remember that he didn't laugh much when I sank a car, or when I skipped school and went hunting or fishing, but he will when Catfish does. I expect that I'll hear him on the sidelines at soccer matches, and in the crowd at school concerts. I'll hear him at the tree house, and out by in the pool. He's always with us at barbecues.

Jennifer will be 24-years-old on Monday, and he would have been 81.

RIP, Daddydoc.

Memories of Christmas Past

I miss them most on Christmas Eve. Every Christmas Eve for my entire life, they came to my parents' house and we had quail for dinner. When he and Dad were younger, they would go quail hunting the morning of Christmas Eve for the quail we would have for dinner that night. They were quail hunting on the day after Christmas in 1960 when I knocked a candle over and burned the house down.

As years passed and we grew from tots to teenagers, they were there every year. Gifts changed from drums and cap guns to duck calls and hunting coats. Many an evening was spent 'practicing' calling ducks with him in the hall at my parents' home. In the summertime, we would walk over to the ponds at the country club at dusk and practice calling the tame ducks there, and sometimes, we'd fish there.

Every year or so, they would go somewhere magical. It might be Hawaii, or Germany, or Spain. They would travel on exciting vacations and live large. All the way from Tunica, Mississippi they traveled the world and saw the sights, heard the sounds, ate the food and drank the liquor.

On Christmas Eve, it was almost like there was assigned seating. Miss Dot always sat at the end of the couch. Smiling and laughing she would tell stories of the hard times in Mississippi. They used to have to travel to Memphis to buy a fifth of whiskey. They would go on Saturday, and that one fifth would last all week. Liberace didn't have anything on her. She would dress to dazzle.

Coachie would be mostly absorbed in whatever football game was being played. If you listened to him, you would learn some absolutely solid football wisdom. He understood more about what was going on down on the field than anyone I ever met, and he could explain it in such a way that a dumb kid could understand it. He was the same with hunting and fishing. He could explain stuff to you so that you knew it, and you knew you knew it, and you understood why it was the way it was. He taught Drivers Ed. He taught me to drive by having me drive his El Camino to Lake Wapanocca so we could go fishing. I was thirty years old before I realized that my brother, my sister and I were the only people on earth who knew him as "Coachie." The rest of the world knew him as Jimmy.

Dad used to hold his ice filled glass up at eye level while pouring bourbon almost as if he were filling to a mark on a beaker. He'd laugh and tell stories about how cold it was, and how deep the snow was in Germany.

Mom always cooked the quail. With a gathering as large as this, it was always a lot of quail. Ralph, the gentleman's gentleman who mom always hired to help her, would sit at the end of the counter 'helping' Mom cook the quail. At the end of the evening, it was always my job to take Ralph home to Florida, his wife.

We don't live on Cardinal Road anymore. New folks own the house. Mom, Dad, Coachie and Miss Dot have moved on to their greater reward, but they are still with us every Christmas Eve. They are in our thoughts and memories, our conversations and our prayers. They are in the photos we bring out. They are in our laughter, and our smiles.

As Miss Dot used to say, "I'll tell you one damn thing… Merry Christmas!"

The Great Quail Hunt

Once I got my driver's license, every Christmas Eve it was my job to go pick up Ralph, and after dinner, to take Ralph home. Ralph was an old guy, and he was a gentleman's gentleman, of sorts. If you ever had a question about manners, Ralph was the guy to ask. He helped my Mother prepare our Christmas Eve dinner of fried quail for more years than I can remember. When I was a kid, Dad and Coachie used to go quail hunting for the Christmas Eve dinner. When we were older, and wild quail got scarce, Ralph and Mom cooked store-bought quail. I used to pick him up at about three in the afternoon. He would walk with tremendous dignity out of his house. He looked so sharp in his tux. James Brown envied Ralph's hair. Even when Ralph got too old to cook with Mom, I still went and picked him up. He sat at the end of the counter and visited with everyone, and afterwards, I took him home. Some folks say it's not Christmas till Hans Gruber falls off Nakatomi Plaza. I used to say it's not Christmas until I pick up Ralph.

At Mom and Dad's house, Ralph would carefully fold his coat, put a crisply starched full apron on, and he and Mom got down to work frying dozens of quail, making giant batches of black eyed peas, candied yams, mashed potatoes, fried okra, cornbread sticks… and on and on and on. An amazing feast was put together while everyone visited. Coachie and I sometimes practiced calling ducks in the hallway. Miss Dot always lit up the room. Dad would smile, and laugh, and have a great time. My brother, my sister and I just took it all in. We had a great time, but it never occurred to us that one day it would fall to us.

Several years ago, Anthony, one of my sister's son-in-laws, revived the old tradition of a Christmas Eve quail hunt. Every year, Uncle Tony, my brother Matt, Anthony, Little Matt, and Little Tony (neither of whom is little anymore) and Owl go quail hunting. My sister fixes a tremendous dinner, and a good time is had by all.

We lived in New Jersey for many years, and now in Florida. I haven't yet participated in the great quail hunt. I hope next year I can, and even if I can't hunt, I want to be there Christmas Eve. Though Ralph, and Mom and Dad, and Coachie and Miss Dot have all gone to their greater reward, I know they won't miss this. If ever there was a night of good spirits, it's Christmas Eve at my sister's house. All the ghosts will be there.

An Afternoon Movie

Many years ago, I took my daughters, ages 3 and 4, to see a movie. I remembered going to movies with my mom when I was a kid. Mom always picked stuff like "The Sound of Music" or "Mary Poppins". Though 'The Sound of Music' eventually became one of my favorite movies of all time, when I was eight years old or so, it sucked. I did not care for it at all. Don't even get me started on "Mary Poppins".

So, I was eager not to repeat my mother's errors in terms of movie choices. It just so happened that a movie was out with Kevin Costner in it. He's a good guy, I thought. He makes good movies, and I was somewhat familiar with the story. This, I thought, was going to be a good time!

So, Jen and Jordan and I went to the Malco Tri-Cinima in Jonesboro….but it wasn't the Tri-Cinima anymore. There were about 10 movie screens available. The three of us walked in, and after an obligatory visit to the restroom, we zeroed in on the concession stand. A large Popcorn and Sprites were ordered. Who the hell knew they sold buttered popcorn by the bushel and Sprite by the gallon? Ok. This is going to be a learning experience.

We wandered down the hall until we came to the 'theater' that was showing our movie. We walked through the dark curtins into the theater. It was tiny, maybe 100 seats. What the hell happened to the giant cavernous rooms they used to show movies in?

We sat down in the center of an empty row in the center of the room. There were eight other people in the room. Most were just a few rows in front of us. We chit-chatted while the 30 minutes of movie previews were shown. The movie trailers were loud and violent and unrelenting. They were everything I would have loved as an eight year old boy, but absolutely not what I was expecting to be previewed while waiting for a kid's movie. I was not pleased with the theater's choices.

Finally, the movie starts. Our hero's father, an English Lord, is penning a letter inquiring about his son who apparently is being held in a prison far, far away when suddenly he is interrupted by a villager in need of assistance with ruffians of some sort. As any good English Lord would do, he donned his armor, mounted his steed and rode out to confront the villager's tormentor. Unfortunately, he was met just outside his castle by a band of armed men who were waiting to attack him.

To say that Jen and Jordan were bothered by this scene is

something understatement. I thought it was a bit violent for a kid's movie. After coxing them out from under the seats, I tried to calm them down and assure them that the bad men were not going to bother Kevin Costner's father. "They just want to talk some", I said.

As the scene shifted to a dark and obviously dangerous prison somewhere, I was having my doubts that this was a kid's movie. One of the guards accused one of the prisoners of stealing bread. As a consequence, the guard was about to cut off the prisoners hand using a sword and a chopping block. CHOP OFF HIS HAND WITH SWORD?

What the hell kind of nut put's this sort of stuff in a kid's movie? It got worse, Kevin Costner, much to my daughter's dismay, took the place of the accused prisoner saying "I'll show you English Courage". The girls turned on the water works. Tears fell like rain. Kevin Costner extended his hand. Between gasps and tears, one of my daughters wailed "He's not gonna cut off Kevin Costner's hand is he?" I was frozen in time. Another guard wrapped a leather strap around Kevin Costner's wrist so he could not movie his hand. "Daddy! Is he going to cut off Kevin Costner's hand?" screamed the girls in unison. The two couples in the rows in front of us began to shuush us. The girls were nearing hysteria. Kevin Costner was about to get his hand cut off! There was no calming them down.

Just as the guard swung the huge sword down toward Kevin Costner's hand, Costner yanked back on the strap really hard. The girls launched a bushel buttered popcorn and two gallons on Sprite high into the air as they flinched in their seats on seeing this. In pulling back like he did, Kevin Costner pulled the other guards hand on to the block and it was summarily cut off by the sword! Kevin Costner then picked up the sword and killed every guard in the room! The girls were under the seats again, wailing like tornado sirens. The folks sitting in front of us were shouting about being covered in popcorn and Sprite.

The movie stopped, lights came on, and with the assistance of the management, we left the movie.

Just an observation: "Robin Hood, Prince of Thieves" is not a child's movie.

My children are grown now, and to this day they refuse to go to movies with me.

Blessings

Every now and then, I pause and count my blessings. I've had a wonderful life. In my time, I have been a cowboy, a carpenter, a diving instructor, a sky diver, and a computer geek. I rode a bull exactly one time. I have had an office in my basement, and I have had an office on the 27th floor above Madison Ave in NYC. I spent twenty-five years in New Jersey and have seen more Yankee baseball games at Yankee Stadium than I can remember. For fifteen years I owned a Jaguar XJS. It is a magical ride. I now live with the girl of my dreams and two dogs in the middle of nowhere in beautiful, sunshiny Florida, in a beautiful house with a pool, a pavilion, and a gun range. I have three wonderful kids who are enjoying life and building successful careers. My grandson literally is chaos.

I think back on how I got here, and invariably I think of my Dad. He was honestly the most amazing person I ever met. He was a doctor in General Practice for sixteen years and practiced radiology for twenty more after that. He delivered more babies in Jonesboro than anyone else in his time as a GP. He used to drive up to Cedar Valley to do physicals for the Boy Scouts every summer. In the early 1960s, he got $25 for delivering a baby at home. I can't count the number of times he sewed me up on the kitchen table.

He was compassionate and caring to everyone, especially strangers. He participated in the community, and helped the YMCA in Jonesboro get its new building built. He loved golf, but didn't have time for it until he retired, and then he just didn't play. He loved to fish, but wasn't very good at it. Patience wasn't one of his strengths. He loved barbeque, football and Ole Miss. He had a circle of friends as wide as the world. He seemed to know everyone, and everyone seemed to know him. I once dated a girl from Paragould. Her father was a banker, a one-eyed banker. We had been dating for several weeks when I found out that Dad was the doctor who removed his eye. I once hit a deer with my truck. The state trooper who wrote up the report looked at me and said, "You Doc's boy?" He knew everyone, and everyone knew him.

My sister was a straight-A student, and Miss Perfect. Sweet Pea could dance like a Russian ballerina or a hot Latina doing the Tango. Just pick the music and she could do the dance. She was as smart as she was beautiful. I remember when Dad got her a super fuzzy deluxe Texas Instruments calculator for some math class she took when she was in high school. I could tell how proud Dad was of her by the way they talked about math. Math was her superpower. He valued intelligence and knowledge over all things and with Sweet Pea he found both.

My little brother was a nationally ranked swimmer, and a basketball phenomenon. While competing at a national level in swimming, he went several years without losing a single race. It was a bad outing if he didn't set a record. We traveled all over the southern United States to the big meets of the time… the Phillips 66 Meet of Champions, the Jr. Olympics in Stillwater, OK., some damn meet in Georgia whose name I can't remember. Like Sweet Pea, he made straight-A's in school. He was Mr. Everything. In the one year he won Cross Country for the State of Arkansas, set the state record for the high jump and was All State in Basketball. Once, I showed him three cords on my guitar. The next summer he and some friends put out a Christian rock album (Fun in the Son) and their band (Manna) went on tour in the South Pacific. His senior year of high school, his high school basketball coach named his first-born son after him. My brother wasn't Jack Armstrong, All American boy. He was Jesus Christ, Superstar.

In every family there is that one kid. In our family it was me. I was Bart Simpson before Bart Simpson was Bart Simpson. There was nothing in which I could not find a bad influence. I used hunting as an escape from school. I got a haircut every six months whether I needed it or not. I was sometimes late for English class due to duck hunting. I learned that blondes really are more fun. I got uncounted cars stuck in every conceivable location while going hunting or trying to get laid. I sometimes enjoyed illegal smiles. I made friends with drunks in Truman to facilitate my bootlegging business. I made A's in chemistry and Physics the same semester that I flunked Algebra II. Algebra was my last class for the day. It interfered with fishing. I squeaked through English Lit, and became a published poet. I worked at Minuteman hamburgers for exactly two weeks before the manager pissed me off and I quit. I bought a bucket and a squeegee. I washed windows for about a dozen businesses to earn my beer and ammo money. I made a habit of breaking my hand for a while. Dad and his friend the orthopedic surgeon (Larry Mahon) would dip water out of the pool for the casting kit to set my hand while enjoying bloody marys on the pool deck. I almost didn't get to participate in the science fair one year because the sheriff confiscated my science fair project. It was a still. Dad wasn't happy, and I made my first trip to the county jail. I almost had a second trip later that year when I got caught stealing the Black Oak, Arkansas population sign. Fortunately the Justice of the Peace let me pay a $25 fine and I got to keep the sign. Early in my Junior year of high school, it was suggested to my parents that I graduate as a Junior as I had become a disruptive influence at school.

Everyone loved Dad because he helped so many people. I have a different view. I remember a man who always gave a screw-up of a kid another chance. He had two high performers and me, but he always believed in me. A friend once commented that my Dad was "awfully hard" on me. That wasn't quite right. He didn't expect anything from me that he didn't expect from Miss Perfect or Jesus Christ. I absolutely was a loose cannon. I was hard on Dad. Being young and dumb, I never realized it, but as a father now I can clearly see it. No matter what I screwed up, he was always there with another chance. I truly and deeply know what unconditional love is because I experienced it time and time again. For no good reason, he always believed in me.

I said all that to say this: Dad was not perfect. As with everyone, he had his flaws. He had some dandies, too. When I remember him to my kids, that's not what I remember. I let his flaws lay silent and dark because they do not do him justice. They were not representative of his character, of what

I learned from him, of what he did for me or of what I want to pass down to my kids and grandchildren. Passing down the lessons from this man does not require that I preface his story with a recitation of his flaws. They know he was human and accept that. I want my progeny to know that he was a good man, a really good man. He encouraged me and my brother to help those who could not help themselves, and defend those who could not defend themselves. By his example, he taught my brother and me to be gentlemen at all times. I may have failed at this on occasion. He unconditionally insisted on fairness and honesty in all things. In his actions and attitudes, my brother, my sister and I learned tolerance by his example. We learned kindness, courtesy and respect by the way he treated my mother. We learned integrity by watching him conduct ordinary business. He was what I wanted to grow up to be.

I can never live up to the standard my father set, but I will never quit trying. (He taught us to be stubborn, too.) I want to pass on to my children all the good qualities my father had, and I want to let his struggles with the realities of the human condition rest in peace. That's not to deny he had flaws. It is to say that I think my offspring are better served by learning about the good things he taught rather than dwelling on the imperfections suffered by a good man.

I think it is important to remember, uphold and honor our parents for the good things they taught us, and blessings they gave to us.

Perhaps, in the interest of harmony, we can grant Washington, Jefferson and the rest of the founding fathers the same courtesy.

The Gift

On Christmas Eve, my brother, sister and I were always very eager to open gifts. Our family tradition was that after dinner we could open one gift. We usually had to wait for a pretty good while after dinner to do it. We just spent a long time with Mom and Dad, and Coachie and Miss Dot laughing and telling stories about Christmases past. We'd all laugh when Coachie would tell the story about how I jumped out of the baby bed when I was five months old. Dad always told the story about when he and Coachie were quail hunting in Dad's MG Midget and they had a flat. Unfortunately, they had no jack. Not a problem, Coachie just picked up the back of the car while Dad changed the tire. On with the hunt! There was always football talk, and if you were wise, you listened carefully to Coachie BEFORE you spoke with your bookie. Before we realized it, it was 10:30 and we'd open gifts before going to midnight services.

So, here we are forty years later. A few years ago, while watching my children open their gifts, I had the most amazing Christmas epiphany. All those years ago, I used to look under the tree at my parents' home at the wondrous array of gifts. I was amazed at the huge number of beautiful gifts that were there. I knew that there would be new clothes and maybe new boots, a new Cowboy hat perhaps, and books. I always got books, and loved every one of them. My brother and sister got similar gifts, all wrapped in festive paper and tied up with ribbons and bows. I thought they were all the most wonderful gifts imaginable, and they were, but I was, nonetheless, wrong.

They say Christmas gifts are for the 'kids' and 'they' are wrong. In a most amazing moment, I realized that the 'gifts' under the tree aren't the 'gifts' at all. The real gift, for parents, is that, even if it's just for one day, the hectic pace of modern life stops for a little while and you get to see your kids smile again. Your children, who are otherwise off building their lives and families, come from far and wide for a special night with you. You hold babies, celebrate career triumphs and commiserate disappointments. You get updates on progress toward life's goals. You hear of loves lost, and exciting new opportunities. No one will be watching Seinfeld reruns tonight! There are gifts to open!

Your children will continue to think that the Christmas gifts are under the tree until their kids go off to college or marry. That is when they will realize that the gifts a parent most cherishes are those precious few hours with their kids. To a parent, getting to spending time with your kid is the gift. The boxes under the tree are just bait.

Go see your parents. No need to wrap a gift.

Merry Christmas!

Friends

In Memory of a Friend

Moments of clarity. Singleness of thought. Focus. In a world broken up into twelve-second sound bites, we have few moments of clarity. We are torn from one screaming crisis to another until something gives us pause, and we take that moment to think.

It is sometimes said that youth is wasted on the young. Youth certainly wasn't wasted on John Moss. Some people burn through life like a comet. Others float and drift like a leaf in the wind. John was a poem.

I met him one morning in the fall of 1980 when I walked out of my rented basement bedroom in Oxford, Mississippi and found him sleeping on the pool table. I woke him and introduced myself. He had driven all the way from Jacksonville to Oxford the night before. We went to Shoney's for breakfast and began a thirty-six-year friendship.

John left us Thursday. He fought the good fight against a relentless cancer for eighteen months. He knew the score from day one, and still he lived every day the good Lord gave him. We visited him six weeks ago in Jacksonville. He was sick. He looked sick.

Sometimes you hear it said that we should strive to be the person our dog thinks we are. John was the guy his dog thought he was. He was kind and gentle. He was generous and compassionate. He was fun and smart. He was caring and thoughtful. He was all this to everyone he ever met. This was John Moss.

We are all better people for having had John in our lives. We are all forever changed for the better by his enthusiasm, his optimism and his laughter. John put a silver lining around every storm cloud he ever saw.

So fare thee well, John Butler Moss… "Hootie." Rest in peace. We will all miss you forever, but we smile and laugh through our tears as we remember the celebration that was your life.

Abbie's Irish Rose

As we progress through Catfish's final semester, I sometimes reminisce some about my final semester before graduation at Ole Miss some 39 years ago. Catfish seems to be approaching graduation in a much more controlled and reasoned manner than I did. He goes out to pubs with friends. They drink beer and talk about job prospects and then they Uber safely home.

Some thirty-nine years ago at Ole Miss, we didn't have Uber. We had Matt. Not my brother, Matt, but an entirely different Matt. Matt somehow became our designated driver. He usually drove when we went to 'Abby's Irish Rose'. Abby's was a bar located beneath an old building in Oxford. It's only access was located in an alley way. Halfway down the alley, there was a lot that once held a building, but the building was long gone and the lot was now a tiny parking lot.

Back in the day, we would all gather at Dave's apartment for late afternoon or early evening libations before climbing into Matt's Mercury Comet for the trip to Abby's. For those who don't know, a Mercury Comet was Lincoln Mercury's take on a Ford Maverick. It was a large, ugly, slow, and cumbersome two door 'swept back, sporty' car. It was built to accomodate four people, two in front and two in back. This car was a sluggish, unbalanced monster to drive. It's only redeeming characteristics were that it was built like a tank and we could stuff six people in that car.

Off we would go to 'Abby's Irish Rose'. We usually tried to leave early enough to guarantee a parking spot in the tiny ally parking lot. Matt would carefully maneuver the beastly car into a tiny spot in the cramped lot, sometimes having to back up, and pull forward several time to get squarely in the parking space. We'd all trot into the pub for several hours of debauchery. Abby's had pool tables in the sub-basement room, and some of us would play for a while. It had a general bar room that opened up to an outdoor patio. After several hours of beer fueled socializing, we'd all stagger back to Matt's sporty Comet for the return ride to Dave's apartment.

One night, we were all crammed in the mighty Comet and ready to repeat the 'backing up a foot, pulling forward a foot' maneuver to extract the car and go home. Matt started the car, and twisted around to see out the back of the car as he turned the steering wheel sharply. He began to gingerly ease out of his parking space. Just as he was applying pressure to the gas pedal, he hiccuped. His foot went down on the gas just a little too hard. The car lurched backward a couple of feet until we heard a solid crunch. We had impacted the Impala parked behind us. We had hit it right smack dab on the door. Being the assholes we were, we found this incredibly funny. We all laughed like hell. Well, everyone except Matt.

"Shit!", Matt muttered, which made us laugh even louder. Apparently, there is nothing funnier than a friend denting cars in a parking lot. He was a bit pissed as he grabbed the shifter and put the car in drive. He cut the steering wheel back some, and, still muttering, he began to ease forward just a bit. Just then, he hiccuped again. The car lurched forward, again ending with a crunch and producing howls of laughter. The car beside us was a Volkswagen. It was now sporting a slightly dented side. We were laughing so hard we were turning blue.

"Oh shit!" he said somewhat excitedly. He quickly jerked the shifter into reverse. Again, looking back out the rear window and about to begin backing up, he hiccuped. We were laughing even before we heard and felt the crunch which sent us deeper into shrieking hysterics. Matt, who was now experiencing an emotional event and was in the grips of blind panic, quickly put the car in drive again. The impala now had a second dent in the door, about a foot away from the first one. Once more, a hiccup produced a crunch as we again hit the VW in front of us, adding a dented fender to the dented side. All of us in the car were about to lose bladder control.

This continued three or four more times with Matt becoming more vocal and more panicked and more agitated with each impact. Finally, Matt successfully extracted the Comet from the tiny parking lot and we returned to Dave's apartment without further incident.

As I think of this incident, I am grateful my son is much more mature than I was, and I thank God for Uber.

A Dog's Life

I first met Nellie when, after drinking for a few hours at CW's house, Landi and I had to attend a function at the Big Fat Head's house. The Big Fat Head was what we called the head of school that our children attended. We had never been to the Big Fat Head's house before. It wasn't hard to find, and we parked among the other cars and walked into the house... the wrong house. Into Brother Jeff's house, who was quite surprised to see us. And we determined at that moment that Nellie was much more of a "greeter" type dog than a guard dog. Nellie was happy to see us too. So after petting Nellie and chatting with Brother Jeff, we left, walked next door, and staggered into the function. We both would have preferred to stay at Jeff's petting his dog and drinking his liquor. Nellie passed away last spring.

Spanky first greeted me with an abrupt package check. I don't remember exactly how many years ago it was, but it certainly caught me by surprise at the Christmas party. I'll not say that he was a chronic crotch sniffer, but I suspect that Spanky became acquainted with everyone at the party. I had a good time watching Spanky do the "nose" thing. The expressions on the faces of the unsuspecting guests were just priceless. Spanky wouldn't be much of a watchdog either. He was happy to see everyone, and I suspect that everyone was happy to see him. Spanky passed away last week.

Buckwheat was imported. He arrived in New Jersey on a flight from Memphis in January of '95. Jordan picked him out of a litter of eight in an Arkansas town so small that the only building in town had collapsed back in the fifties and no one had bothered to build it back... but this place was still a town. Just ask either of the people who lived there. Buck lived a life of leisure. He used the pool more than any of us. He took naps wherever and whenever he wanted to. He taught Catfish to pee in the yard, and to turn around three times before laying down for a nap. He did make it tough to potty-train Catfish. According to Catfish, it was Buckwheat who was putting poop in his diaper. Buck passed away in September.

Someone once said that if we are lucky, we find maybe two good friends in the course of our lives. I am quite sure that this person never had a dog. Nellie, Spanky, and Buck all were our good friends. They listened to us when we needed to talk. They comforted us when we were sad. They danced through our lives without ever contemplating their own mortality, and left us with only smiles and fond memories.

Let us each strive to be the person these great friends thought that we were. May they rest in peace.

Old Friends and Memories

As the holidays approach, we are planning a visit to Jonesboro, Arkansas, my hometown. I always look forward to visiting home. With each visit, some friend of mine sees fit to tell my wife, Landi, yet another "Bill story." Some are quite entertaining and many are grossly exaggerated. Let's just say there are few things left that will shock her and it seems pretty damn clear that I should never, ever run for public office. I have a number of friends who maintain that I have never been accused of doing something that I didn't actually do.

Sometimes, you see an old friend, and for some reason, you just don't recognize the person. This happened several years ago at my mother's funeral. My sister, my brother and I were greeting people after they paid their last respects to Mom at the funeral home. Mom had a lot of friends, many of whom I have not seen in twenty or twenty-five years. Most had a "Bill story" for us to suffer through. We all had some pretty good laughs about cars and some of the things I did years ago. There are a lot of "Bill stories" out there. Not all of them are me. Some are really "Matt stories" but it's just more believable when folks say it was me.

At some point about halfway through the viewing, a strikingly beautiful woman entered the room. She didn't walk. She flowed into the room as if she were borne on a breeze. She greeted and chatted with my sister. She spoke briefly with my brother. They seemed to know her. She approached me and paused, smiling. I smiled back. She stuck her hands out, and I took both her hands in mine. I looked back at her beautiful eyes, wondering for all the world who in the hell this woman was. For just a moment she looked deeply into my eyes. She winked at me and leaned in close. I broke a sweat. She whispered in my ear, "Bill, do you know what we share?"

Oh God.

This woman was clearly too beautiful to have engaged in debauchery with me back in the day, but I had debauched a lot back in the 1970s. I was getting dizzy. The room was starting to spin. I was going into brain lock. I couldn't breathe. I couldn't move. I could feel my wife's eyes burning a hole in the side of my head. Really? We "share" something? Wonder what that could be?

She could tell I was surprised. She smiled again; her eyes twinkled as she casually brushed a few stray strands of hair from her face. She laughed and playfully slapped me on the arm.

"Oh silly!" she said, smiling, almost laughing. "We share a birthday!"

Thank you, Jesus.

At that moment, I knew who this beautiful woman was.

First Love

She was my very first love and it was late afternoon when she called. It had been a long, hard day, but I knew she would call, and I knew that I would answer. We had spoken earlier, and agreed that it would be a good thing to meet later. This was that call.

I drove slowly to the rendezvous point. On the way, it occurred to me that I had known her my entire life, but only in the context of the people we were about to visit. We all had been at this very same spot only a few hours before. She and Larry were already there when I arrived. Together, the three of us walked across the Veterans section of the cemetery to the fresh grave site where he rested beside his wife, Miss Dot.

I scanned the evening sky as if looking for ducks, and pulled a silver flask from my coat pocket. I offered it to her and could not help but see the sadness in her eyes. She took it, and slowly unscrewed the cap. Larry and I just watched her. She looked so tired as she carefully poured a bit of bourbon out on to the ground. A lone tear wandered down her cheek as she toasted her father one last time.

Larry and I each took our turns with the flask, and both of us offered a toast to the man resting in the grave before us.

In the 1960s, my brother and I used to tell folks we knew the strongest man in the world and that his name was Coachie. He was strikingly handsome, the living embodiment of a true southern gentleman. He spent countless hours during my childhood teaching me the finer points of duck calling, a skill which I have spent a life time exploiting.

The walk back to the cars was long, and slow. Darkness had fallen. As we approached the cars, she stopped and asked me, "Is there anything of Daddy's that you would like?"

"Yes," I replied. "I would like that old Olt duck call. It was the call he taught me to call on." The don't make them anymore.

"It's yours," she said. She began to turn as if to get in the car, but she stopped and turned back to me. She paused for a second and asked me a second question.

"Is there anything your brother would like?"

"Yes," I said, "there is."

"What is it?" she countered.

"He would like to be able to call ducks."

Duck Hunting

As we approach duck season, my bride and I are considering sending our son, Catfish, down to Arkansas for a Thanksgiving duck hunt with my brother Matt, his son also named Matt, and Uncle Tony. My brother, my nephew and my brother-in-law have a duck club complete with flooded woods, a blind, and most importantly, a clubhouse with a wet bar, leather couches, Persian rugs, Direct TV and a 60-inch flatscreen television. I am a little concerned because while Matt, Matt 2.0 and Tony are great guys, and they will take great care of Catfish, they cannot call ducks for shit. I have a good friend named John David who is a great guy and who is an excellent duck caller. Perhaps a call to John is in order.

John and I used to hunt a slough in the Cache River bottoms which meant that we had to weave our way in a 14ft aluminum Jon Boat loaded with guns, decoys, beer, and Duke the dog through a tree studded swamp just to get to the slough. Once on the slough, we had to put the decoys out, and then wrestle the boat back into the brush so the ducks wouldn't see it, but not so far as to block either our field of vision or the dog's. If Duke couldn't see the ducks fall, he wouldn't know to go get them.

Usually, we'd get some ducks and have a good time. Sometimes, if the ducks weren't flying, we'd just sit there and drink beer. Sometimes, we'd do both. Once, a bottle of wine got spilled in the bottom of the boat, and Duke lay there lapping it up. A little while later, when one of us shot a duck, Duke was too drunk to go get it so we had to get the boat out of our hide, and go get the duck. This happened several more times, and pissed John off greatly. Each time we'd kill a duck, Duke would just lay there and growl.

Finally, John and I had enough of the attitude from the damn dog. Dogs that can't hold their liquor should not drink. We collected our decoys and headed toward the landing. John was steering the boat, and I complained to him that we were going too fast through the trees. I was afraid we would hit one. We had a 9.8 HP Mercury motor on the fourteen-foot Jon Boat, and even with the load we had in the boat, we were moving pretty damn fast. John, being fortified by having been drinking beer all day, was very dismissive of my concerns and supremely confident in his ability not only to guide the boat but also to judge whether or not the boat would fit between any two given trees. We were simply flying through the swamp. I'm in the front of the boat scared stiff as we pass closer and closer to trees, or squeeze between two trees standing close together. Duke is passed out in the bottom of the boat. Decoys are clattering as we shift and weave between the flooded oak trees. The motor is going flat out, and I can hear John laughing over the roar of the motor when suddenly everything stopped.

Well, almost everything. The boat and motor stopped. Everything else including me, my gun, the decoys, the cooler, 100,000 beer cans, John, his gun, and Duke the dog continued moving through the air at pretty much the same rate of speed we were traveling before the boat got stuck. I made out the best because, sitting in the front of the boat, there was nothing for me to hit on the way out of the boat and into the cold, cold water. Duke bounced off the front seat of the boat and then into the water. John hit the middle seat, then the front seat, then hit the water. I was cold and wet. John was cold, wet, and a little dazed. Duke was pissed, and was trying to bite me and John. He may have accidentally eaten a decoy. While I was trying to evade Duke, I stepped into someone's lost trap. The steel jaws slammed into both sides of my ankle, and, even though my boots, hurt like hell. While Duke was chasing John around the swamp, I cut the rope that secured the trap. I told John that I was going to kill whoever owned the trap. I pried the trap from my foot, and checked the tag. It said "Bill Garner/John David."

Finally, we got Duke calmed down and back in the boat. We spent probably an hour splashing around collecting decoys, beer cans, coolers, guns and dead ducks. Finally, we set about getting the boat unstuck from between the trees. It is not possible to convey in words how cold we were. It was early December and a north wind was blowing through the swamp. However, as with most things, un-sticking the boat was, in the end, simply a matter of motivation. After an hour or so of struggle, we were finally successful in freeing the boat, and we motored back to the truck.

On second thought, Catfish might be better off hunting with Matt and Tony.

The First Barbeque

I've been asked a number of times about how I got started doing barbecue. As best as I can remember, this is how it happened. I'm not saying this is one hundred percent accurate, but this is my story, and I'm sticking to it.

When I was about sixteen or seventeen, the man who took care of my dad's cattle had a stroke and died. Dad took advantage of this opportunity to exile me to a cattle farm located sixteen miles north on Jonesboro Arkansas, on highway 141. I was responsible for two hundred head of registered Brangus cattle.

So, I'm living in a trailer on a hill in the boondocks of Arkansas with two hundred expensive ass cattle, and the county line beer joint is only two miles away by way of my pastures. Not a bad setup, if I do say so myself. I used to ride my horse to the beer joint, but that's a whole other story.

So, late one night I was driving back to the farm when something ran out of the woods and I hit it. Whatever it was flew up and over my truck, and I skidded to a stop. I got out and ran back to see what I had hit. It was a deer... a doe. She wasn't dead, so I went back to my truck, got my pistol, and shot her to put her out of her misery. I made a call on my CB radio and asked whoever answered me to call the State Police so I could get an accident report.

It wasn't long before an Arkansas State Trooper pulled up. He was a big guy. He first looked at my truck, and asked if I was hurt. I told him I wasn't. He went over to the deer. He looked down at her, and then he looked at me and said, "This deer has a gunshot wound."

I had to explain that the deer wasn't killed by the impact, so I shot her to put her out of her misery. He was cool with that. After that, we got down to business. I gave him my license. He looked at it and said, "Boy, are you Doc's boy?"

I said, "Yes sir."

Nothing much else was said until the trooper asked me what I was going to do with the deer. I told him that I was going to have a party. I told him I figured I'd cook it the next day. With that, he gave me my accident report. I loaded the deer in the back of my truck, and the trooper drove off.

The next morning, I called a few friends, and invited them over for a barbecue. Johnny made a run to the line and got a quarter keg of beer. Barry showed up with some tequila. Slater arrived with bourbon. I got the backhoe and dug us a pit. We built a fire, and used the headache rack of the dozer to hold the deer. We settled in for some serious drinking and shooting. Did I mention that we had a bunch of guns?

Living out in the boonies and having access to a bulldozer provides certain opportunities. One of these is the ability to construct a shooting range. I had cleared a shooting range down a draw with barrels set at 100, 150 and 300 yards. I had some short targets at 25 and 50 feet for pistols. Let me say now, that there is nothing in this world that is more fun than handguns and tequila. We shot for a while, then went back to the fire and the keg.

Me, Johnny, Barry and Slater are sitting there talking and drinking, and reflecting on how life just doesn't get any better than this when suddenly, with not a word of explanation, they all jumped up, sprinted across the corral, jumped the fence, and disappeared into the woods. Even being drunk, I knew this was odd behavior, so I looked behind me.

Three Arkansas State Police cars were pulling into the drive.

I was sixteen or seventeen years old, in possession of a keg of beer, a couple bottles of whiskey and tequila, about a dozen weapons, an untagged, out of season deer on the grill... and I was drunk.

So, I figured it was a pretty sure thing that I was going to jail.

Wrong! The Trooper who did my accident report had come over and brought a couple of friends to the barbecue. As they made a beeline to the keg, I realized that they had come to party, so I started showing off the attractions. First, I showed them the horses. We had six, and I figured they might want to ride. Then I showed them my shooting range. I was a little nervous about showing them the weapons, because a few of them may not have been legal. One of the troopers took a great deal of interest in the weapons. I was nervous. I didn't want to lose a weapon, so I took a 30-30 and started demonstrating my shooting ability. I thought I was pretty impressive. Apparently, I wasn't.

One of the troopers went back to his car. He came back with a very impressive rifle, equipped with a very impressive scope, and the fun began.

While all this shooting was going on, one by one, Johnny, Barry and Slater all came back in from the woods. I guess all the gunfire was a good sign to them. So they came back and I introduced them to my new friends the State Troopers. We drank beer and shot weapons all afternoon while the deer cooked. When we finally ate, we were out of ammo, and damn near out of beer, so Barry and one of the State Troopers made a beer run. It was clear to all of us that if you have to make a beer run after you've been drinking for about seven or eight hours, it's best if you have a State Trooper drive. They rarely get pulled over.

It was a couple of days later that I realized that barbecuing was a lot of fun. Hell, it's fun even if you don't drink heavily and play with guns.

So, that was the very first barbecue that I was responsible for.

Brisket

My chocolate Lab, Svatchime, watched me warily all day long. In the pre-dawn hours, I carefully built my fire. The Big Green Egg came to easily to temperature. My brisket had sat overnight, salted and peppered, on a rack in the beer fridge. It was dry and looking good when I put it on the Egg. Four hours passed, and I foiled the brisket. I placed my temperature probe into the thickest portion of the brisket. Back into the Egg the brisket went. The wait began. Svatchime and I keep a close eye on the temperature in the Egg as well as the temperature of the brisket. Both are key metrics in the production of a brisket. The Egg temp hovered around 225, and the internal temp of the brisket rose until it stalled at 178. This isn't unexpected. It happens every time.

"Why's it taking so long?", asked Svatchime as if on que.

Yes. My dog talks, but she doesn't have a good memory for details.

Just like every time before, I explained that when a brisket hits the 'stall' its actually doing magic that transforms it from a leathery hunk of tough, grainy near rawhide meat into an amazing chunk of mouth watering beef. We'll keep the brisket on the Egg and not let the internal temp of the brisket exceed 203. We'll hold it at 203 for about four hours, for about an eight or ten hour total cook time.

"I can't wait to taste it", Svatchime said as she sat drooling in the shade.

"No brisket for you", I replied. "Remember, brisket and you do not get along", I added. A chill ran up my spine, and for just a minute I could not see out of one eye.

Some five years ago, I barbequed 5 huge briskets for a local fire company celebration. I cooked them at home, and planned to deliver them the next day. Brisket cooking is a long and tiresome task, and once it is done you are exhausted. On this occasion, I pulled the briskets at about 10:00PM. I wrapped them in foil, and placed them on the counter in the kitchen to cool for a few hours before I put them on ice. I lay down and rested.

I woke up at 5:00AM, and went down to the kitchen to stow the briskets. Where I had left five briskets the night before, there now were only four. Where Svatchime the night before had been full of energy and a pain in the ass, now she lay on the floor with an amazingly distended belly, surrounded by the remnants of foil. She had consumed an entire 17lb brisket. She was too full to move. She moved only her eyes as she watched me explode.

So I kicked Svatchime out of the house and cleaned up the kitchen floor. I was furious. I delivered the remaining brisket to the firehouse and spent the rest of the day cleaning the kitchen floor again because briskets give up a lot of grease.

That evening, we had guests. One was a dear friend from just a block over, and the other was a friend from our church. Her father was the retired priest of the church. Both are dignified young ladies who are a lot of fun to be around. Both are somewhat prim and proper, but hey…they were coming over to play poker. They are fun people.

They arrived on time. Landi, our guests and I sat down around a small gaming table. Everyone greeted Svatchime and Chaunti. Svatchime lay down behind our guests. Chaunti was in Landi's lap. We began to play poker and chat. We had been playing for about thirty minutes when something went awry, badly awry.

The preacher's daughter suddenly sat up very straight, almost as if she had been shocked. Her eyes sprung wide open and bulged out. Her eye brows leaped onto the top of her head, and steam appeared to emerge from her ears. She began to fan her face very fast and frantically. The neighbor from around the block just stared at her, as did Landi and I. Then she went pale, and pulled her shirt up over her mouth and nose. Her eyes were tearing up, and she went flush. The creases fell from her pressed pants and the colors in her blouse went gray. She began to hyperventilate. She looked about frantically for an escape route.

Landi and I only wondered what was going on for a matter of seconds. Our friends had been the first victims of Svatchime's brisket fart. We were doomed just like them, but we didn't know that as we watched our friends descend into a hypoxic state and enter a near death realm.

Svatchime's fart made it to us. To say it was a smell is to say that Noah and the Ark survived a heavy dew. The air shimmered as the fart approached us. I saw it. Landi saw it. We didn't know what it was. Chaunti knew what gas going on. She leaped from Landi's lap and fled the room. We should have run. We just didn't know that the olfactory insult that was approaching us would render mute, us blister our eyes, and cauterize our noses. The air was perceptibly warmer and more dense inside the fart cloud. The room began to spin as our oxygen deprived brains began their shutdown sequences. Landi, in one last heroic effort, lit a candle.

We survived. We all survived. I kicked Svatchime's ass outside for a week.

After five years, the damn dog remembered how much she like brisket. She was begging for brisket. Just a bite…one bite. One little bite. With her ears on the back of her head, and her eyes locked on mine she said, "One bite…..please… one tiny bite…."

I folded. I gave her a bite.

Two hours later, my generosity was rewarded with a fart that has necessitated repainting the house.

Randoms

The Old Man at White Horse Tavern

He was old and broken, but unbowed in his wheelchair. The lady who brought him in could have been his daughter, but she wasn't. She was very pretty. For several weeks I watched her wheel him in for lunch each Wednesday at the White Horse Tavern. That's the bar in the Village, NYC where Dylan Thomas died.

The old man had long white hair that hung to his shoulders, and he sat erect in his wheelchair; a proud man. He had lost the use of his right arm and leg, to a stroke I supposed. I had to look closely, but I saw that he had a glass eye. I wondered who he was, because clearly, he was somebody. For weeks I sat on my perch in Dylan Thomas' spot, and watched them converse over lunch. Eventually I moved to the table beside the one they always dined at because I wanted to meet this man and this woman. There was something interesting here. I just knew it. Finally, one Wednesday we spoke.

She was from a publishing family in Jackson, Mississippi, and her father-in-law, the Colonel, was a retired Marine Corps pilot. Every Wednesday she picked him up at his apartment, and they would enjoy lunch and cocktails at the White Horse. He loved getting out, rain or shine. I looked kindly at the old man, and I asked him what kind of plane he flew.

He turned a little in his chair to face me more directly, as if he were sizing me up. Then he looked straight into my eyes. Even old and crippled, and stuck in a wheelchair, he was an impressive man, and I realized that he was still a Marine. He flew Corsairs in the South Pacific, he said in a strong voice that pierced the low lunch crowd murmur as easily as machine gun bullets cut through a cloud. The sheer strength and resonance of his voice caught the attention of the guys sitting at the table next to me.

"Do you know where Guadalcanal is?" the old Marine asked me. The ears of the guys sitting at the bar behind him perked up at the mention of Guadalcanal. They turned so they could see the old man as they began to listen surreptitiously. He spoke like it was yesterday, flying force protection for the P-38 Lightnings that shot down General Yamamoto's transport plane. He used words that painted a picture of the blue sky and the damp green jungle covering the island floating on the turquoise sea below. He gestured a little with his left hand as if it were a plane. If you closed your eyes you could see the fight unfold. P-38s, forked tail devils painted that drab Army green, doggedly pursued, dipping and dodging the blue and white transport plane, ripping it apart with machine gun fire while the Colonel and his fellow Marines, in their beautiful blue Corsairs, engaged the Japanese fighters that had been tasked with protecting the General. With a trace of sadness in his voice that only a pilot can produce, he described the transport plane, smoking, spiraling down and exploding on the jungle canopy below.

The story continued, and one by one the patrons at the bar surrendered to the strong voice from the old man in the wheelchair. He stayed in the Corps after the war, and eventually went to Korea. The lunch crowd grew quiet as patrons at nearly every table paused their conversations, leaned back so they could see the old man and hear his story. With the whole tavern his prisoner and in the quiet clear voice of a proud Marine, he told the story of the destruction of the bridges at Toko-Ri. "The movie," he said, "used Jets, but we used Corsairs. Jets went too fast and couldn't get low enough in the canyon. We got our asses shot up, but we got the damn bridges."

I looked at the woman with him. She smiled a smile that told me we were hearing from the young Marine trapped in the old man's broken body. Following Korea, he transitioned into Jets. Over North Vietnam, his jet was shot to pieces, his canopy shot away. He smiled at me, and pulled his long white hair back revealing a mangled ear and massive scars on his head and neck. With his good eye he winked and said, "I caught a little bit of the flak over Hai Phong."

"Oh my God!" I spontaneously said. "You bailed out over North Vietnam?"

He glared at me as if I had uttered blasphemy. His one good eye fixed on me as if a gunsight, and I froze. I just knew he was going to rise up out of that chair and pound me to pulp. He paused and surveyed the lunch crowd standing silenced, transfixed. For the first time he realized that the room was his, that everyone had been captured by his tale. The icy gaze of his pale blue eye, burning with the strength, courage, and discipline of a proud US Marine, returned to me. In voice that echoed in the silent bar, the Colonel said, "My Government sent me out with their goddamned airplane and I brought their goddamned airplane back."

Blind in one eye, and with a mostly useless right arm, he landed his crippled jet on the deck of a pitching carrier in a rainstorm at night on the Gulf of Tonkin.

The room was silent for a few, long seconds, then one man stood and clapped. Another man stood, came to attention, and saluted. One by one, the whole New York City lunch crowd stood and applauded the old man in the wheelchair. The old man looked a little surprised by the response. The Colonel, his right arm laying useless at his side, returned the salutes with a nod.

A few minutes later, his daughter-in-law asked for the check.

"Lady, that tab has already been paid," the bartender replied.

I love New York.

Just Another Dad ....for a day

It was ten years ago, and it was hot. Even for Fall Fair, it was a hot day. I was cooking ribs on my smoker, and I saw him. Something made me look up, and I saw him park his Range Rover and get out. He was in jeans and a t-shirt and he wore a ball cap. He wasn't in disguise. I knew who he was the instant I saw him. He got a worn folding chair from the back of the dusty Range Rover, and walked slowly, nonchalantly across the parking lot to the soccer field. He didn't look about. He didn't greet anyone. He didn't have an entourage. It was just him, and he didn't stop for a Coke, or a hotdog. He just went to the soccer field. Others saw him, too, and they looked briefly so as not to be rude, and then looked away and went back to what they were doing.

It was a good soccer match. I don't remember who won. I took a break from cooking ribs so I could watch the game. In all, there were probably seventy-five parents watching. We cheered and groaned as dictated by the game. The boys played hard, and then the game was over.

He folded his chair, and waited unnoticed in a small crowd of parents waiting for his son to come over for a post-game greeting. Other parents milled about, some waiting for the same purpose. The coaches did their post-game commentary, and the players of both teams trotted over to their parents. By this time, word had spread that he was here, but still he stood alone in a crowd. His son and a couple of friends came to him. They spoke, and laughed, and smiled, and then the boys trotted back over to the bench, and he walked slowly across the field to the parking lot. He put his folding chair in the back of his Range Rover and got in. He drove away.

Sometimes we forget that even rock stars have kids, and sometimes they need to be just another dad. On this day, Wardlaw's whole community of baby boomers and aging hippies stood back and let a rock star be just another dad for a day. The man got to watch his kid play soccer and no one bothered him. No one asked him for a photo. No one asked him for an autograph. No one spoke to him at all. That was the day Bruce Springsteen came to The Wardlaw Hartridge School, and if only for that day, got to be just another dad watching his kid play soccer.

The Saucon Valley Country Club

As we continue to rehabilitate the basement from water damage incurred during August's hurricane, I am finding interesting items long forgotten and stored in remote regions of the basement. With each item, there is usually some memory attached that brings a smile.

The other day, in the back of the storage room in the basement, I came across Landi's golf clubs. When we were dating, we used to play frequently, but we haven't played for years. Her clubs were in the corner of the storage room and I checked the bag for water damage. As I inspected the bag, a smear of mud caught my eye on the shoulder strap, and I remembered the last time we played golf.

In the Lehigh Valley of Pennsylvania, there is a wonderful Country Club called Saucon Valley. It is a beautiful, high-end country club that, were Landi not associated at the time with Bethlehem Steel, we would never have had occasion to visit or play. However, through a Bethlehem Steel event of some sort, we found ourselves at this incredible golf course.

Landi was beautiful that day. She was wearing white shorts and a blue knit top of some sort. She had a white visor, and white golf shoes. Her golf bag was white, as was her golf glove. She had her hair in a pony tail, and a late summer tan. I wore dockers and a polo shirt.

Saucon Valley's course is one of those courses where the fairways are better than a lot of greens that I grew up playing on. We played our round with another twosome associated with Bethlehem Steel. They were much better golfers than us, but we were better looking.

The 18th hole was a long, downhill dog-leg par four, with a small stream crossing at the bottom of the valley. Both of the other golfers in our foursome drove over the stream and into perfect position. I barely cleared the stream, and Landi came up short. I drove her to her ball, and she asked me to go ahead and find my ball, that she would walk to me. I drove the cart to the little bridge over the stream and began looking for my ball.

Landi swung, and her ball flew towards the green. I still couldn't find my ball. I saw the other two golfers waiting, so I told them to go ahead and hit. I had lost a couple of balls already, and I didn't think I had another with me. So I kept looking for it, and I looked up just in time to see Landi kind of hop over the stream. It was a short hop. An easy hop, really. Actually, it was more of a long stride with just a little extra oomph at the end, and she very gracefully cleared the stream without any distress at all.

The ground on the side she was coming from was firm, solid and dry. The other side of the stream was not. It was utterly saturated. Her lead foot landed on the soft green grass, and she sank up to her knee in muck. Her trailing leg completed the stride across the stream, and had no place to go but also knee deep into the muck. Up till this point, only her golf shoes were muddy.

I viewed this from a short distance away, and immediately came to her assistance. I remembered the old Tarzan movies where one guy stuck in quicksand quickly drags another to his doom when he is pulled into the quicksand. No way, I thought, I was getting into the mud.

All things considered, at this point, Landi was doing well. She was stuck in the mud yes, but she was calm. I grabbed a golf club to use to help pull her out. By having her grab the golf club, and using it to pull her out, I hoped to be able to stay on solid ground, and avoid the mud. She took hold of the club and I started pulling, but the mud on her hands caused her to lose her grip. Because she was pulling so hard, when the club slipped out of her hands, she flopped backwards and sat down in the mud. As she lost her grip, I was straining, pulling the club trying to lift her out. Suddenly losing that resistance, my hands, clutching the head of the 3-iron, crashed into my nose, which began bleeding profusely.

I ventured closer, and extended my hand to her, and again we pulled and strained. The grass beneath my feet gave way, and suddenly, I was flat on my back in the mud. Landi's calm was wearing thin. I got up, grabbed her under the arms, and using brute strength, tried to lift her out of the mud, and again, my feet slipped in the mud and I went down. I sat down in front of her, reached out to her, and tried again. Her leg was slowly coming free, and suddenly she shouted, "STOP!"

"What's wrong?" I asked.
"I'm losing my shoe!!"
"Screw the shoe. I'll get the shoe in a minute."

We kept pulling and straining and after a great sucking/slerping sound, her foot came free, and we rolled onto more firm grass. We were tired, exhausted really. Finally, after catching our breath, I started to head to the golf cart.

"My shoe...?" Landi reminded me.

I walked back over to the mud pit we had created. It was a hell of a mess. The groundskeeper was going to wonder what the hell happened here. I found the hole. I got on my knees, and stuck my arm down until I felt the golf shoe. I pulled it out of the muddy water, held it aloft, and watched as what looked like Hershey's syrup poured from it. I looked over at Landi, and she looked like she had been dipped in Hershey's syrup. I had to smile.

The other two players in our foursome had finished the hole, and were sitting on the patio at the clubhouse when we arrived. When they last saw us, we looked like we could have been in a photo shoot for a golf magazine, but that had changed. Both of us were covered from head to toe in a dark brown mud, and were coated with an abundance of grass clippings. The blood spatters from my nose on my shirt and pants just added a special ambiance.

I wish I had a picture of the looks on their faces, and the faces of the others at the patio bar. This is one of the most exclusive country clubs in the United States, and this golf course has hosted many a PGA and LPGA event. We walked dripping mud and trailing grass trimmings into the patio bar, and sat with our friends, who had a truly horrified look on their face. They were staring, slack-jawed and silent.

The manager approached, looking very apprehensive.

"Can I help you?" he inquired.

I wiped at my nose and looked to see if it was still bleeding. "Tough hole," I said casually.

The Van

Last year's Christmas adventure began with the van breaking down due to water in the fuel in the middle of a freezing rainstorm. We were rescued by my father-in-law, who loaned us his minivan. We celebrated our good fortune by slamming the car door on my hand. On our return trip, we rapped both of my shins with an ironing board.

This year, events in Arkansas dictated that we make a quick, unplanned trip there. The trip began most innocently enough on a beautiful day. We thought that we had successfully sat out the bad weather that had occurred south of us. We were wrong.

It began as snow "flurries" and ended as a "winter storm." Not just any winter storm, a major winter storm that knocked power out all over southern Virginia.

We hung tough, and drove carefully past twenty-five wrecked cars. We saw cars in ditches. We saw cars in the median. We saw cars balanced on the guard rails. We saw ten cars crashed on an icy bridge at mile marker 105. The van proved steady as we drove at 35-40 miles-per-hour, staying on the ruts in the snow.

There is a good bit of stress that goes along with driving 330 miles in a storm that is going from snow to ice. As we began to escape the snow, though tired, I thought, "Dang... we're going to make it."

Ahhh... ye of little faith. Just like Janet Leigh stepping into the shower in Psycho, just like the Skipper and Gilligan, just like George Clooney sailing out of Gloucester Harbor... when we got into the van on that beautiful morning in Jersey, we were doomed. Janet got slashed and stabbed. The Skipper and Gilligan were stuck on an island. George drowned in the North Atlantic. We, we were screwed.

The van farted... and farted again... and again. DAMN! Water in the damn fuel. We limped to the frozen rest area. I poured STP gas treatment in the tank just in time for the motor to die.

We're screwed. Landi looked at me. I looked at her. We looked around at the ice-covered trees, and the ice coated sidewalks. It was dusk and we were in a rest area on I-81 just north of Marion, Virginia in the middle of a horrible ice storm. We called the State Police, and they said they would dispatch a trooper as soon as they could. We could hear sleet hitting the van, and we could see the icicles growing longer.

Because we expected it to take hours for the trooper to arrive, we climbed into the back of the van. The huge captains chairs are much more comfortable than the driving compartment. Using ice from the storm, I fixed cocktails as Miss Landi prepared hors d'oeuvres.

We were sitting in relative comfort enjoying the storm when suddenly, there was a rapping on the window, and a flashlight lit the interior of the van. It was the state trooper. It only took one hour for him to arrive.

Once he overcame the initial shock of seeing people climb out of the back of an ice covered, stranded van clutching cocktails, the trooper was very helpful and called for a tow truck. We climbed back into the van for more cocktails and snacks.

Roughly forty-five minutes later the tow truck arrived, and we were rescued. The truck operator dropped us at the only hotel in the area that still had power. We disembarked clutching all manner of crap. We had fur coats. We had computers. We had the port-a-bar.

When at last we entered our warm and dry hotel room, we deposited our gear and discovered something.

Make a note. When stranded for any reason, don't forget to get the luggage out of the car before they tow it to the garage.

I don't have to make a note. I'm sure my bride will always remind me.

It was an Ordinary Road Trip

We set out at about 9:00AM on December 26th for a long anticipated trip to Arkansas. Because we planned to hunt, we had guns. Because it was our Christmas visit, we had gifts. Because we would be gone a week, we had tons of luggage. Because we're stupid, we had a dog. We were packed pretty tightly in the van when we set off in the rain and wind and cold.

Things went relatively well for about an hour, when it appeared that we had encountered bad gas. No, not that gas. Gas that makes the van go. So, at Hellertown, PA, we pulled off the road, bought some Gas-Dry, and filled the tank with more gas. We started the van... well, we tried to start the van. Of course, the damn van wouldn't start.

Fortunately, my father-in-law lives only a couple of miles away, and there happened to be a tow truck sitting at the gas station, so we had the van towed, and switched our 'stuff' to my father-in-law's minivan. Did I mention that we did all this in a cold, blowing rain? You're probably thinking something like "this can't get worse."

Oh, ye of little faith. It can always get worse. Think about how your hands feel when they are cold, and wet. Really, really, really cold. Now, slam the car door on one of your hands. See, it can be worse. Fortunately, no great harm came from the experience. My hand is fine.

So we traveled to Arkansas in a minivan full of guns, luggage, dogs, gifts and us, and it really wasn't a bad trip.

In Arkansas we prepared for our duck hunt. Because the water was so high, we had to go out in the swamp in the boat to collect and re-position the decoys. So, we're in a 14 ft. Jon Boat, in a swamp that normally is about two feet deep in water, but is now about five feet deep, and of course, we foul the prop on the motor with the rope. Did I mention that it's cold, the wind is blowing, and that we are in a swamp that is too deep to walk out of, about a mile from the landing... and now the boat motor won't go? Fortunately, we are able to maneuver to a place where my nephew is able to stand on a floating tree, and, using my knife, clear the prop. We motored out.

The hunt the next day was equally interesting. Because there's so much water, the ducks have too many choices and stayed away from us. On the way out, we pulled up to the duck clubhouse, were about to tie off the boat, and go in. My niece's boyfriend was struggling with tying off the boat, so I stood up and stepped out of the boat to walk around to the front to tie it for him. The nice thing about the clubhouse is that it is situated so that we usually can motor right up to a really shallow spot, and just step out of the boat into about six inches of water. The operative word is "usually." Not always. Not when the water is up by four feet. Then the water is four feet, six inches deep. Yeah, it's cold, too.

Finally, after spending a week in Arkansas visiting friends and family, we headed home. We covered seven hundred miles on the first day, and were well pleased with our progress. We had a great supper from Ruby Tuesday, and slept well. At about 5:30 am, I woke up and walked to the bathroom.

Apparently, at some point in the night, my darling wife morphed into Cato from the Pink Panther movies. So that our yappy little dog could not approach the door of the hotel room, she had placed the ironing board on its side, on the ground to form a "fence" of sorts, blocking the dog's access to the door. Half asleep, and in the dark, I rediscovered the ironing board with my foot. I fell forward, catching my upper body with my hands, and rapping both shins very sharply on the narrow metal edge of the ironing board. Both shins. Two-hundred-and-twenty-six pounds of falling, middle aged, hypertensive redneck landing on my shins on a narrow metal ironing board. Let that soak in for a minute. In the truest sense of the word, it is a whole new kind of pain.

Happy New Year

Superbowl

January 15, 2009

Super Bowl T-minus sixteen days:

The day began normally, but ended with a one-inch stream of water pouring into the basement from an electrical conduit. Yes... an electrical conduit. Who the hell do you call for that? A plumber or an electrician? Together, my wife and I fought the water. A plumber came and capped the electric conduit. We are standing in 3-4 inches of water and as he cuts each wire, he says, "Watcha for da sprarka." I'm thinking, this may very well become an example of natural selection.

The water company arrives and shuts the water off. It's four degrees outside. I'm pumping water from the basement but the hose keeps freezing up. Each time I go outside to clear it, my hand freezes to the metal door knob when I re-enter the house.

January 16, 2009

Super Bowl T-minus fifteen days:

The water is turned off. We begin a four-day marathon of drying out the basement. The big screen is intact and functional. Damage appears to be minimal. The Middlesex Water Company bozos begin maneuvering to avoid paying for repairing the water line. They forgot to bill us for our "Customer Care Line Protection." Our homeowner's insurance begins trying to tell me that this is ground water (not covered). I calmly explain that in my experience, I have always seen water flow from a pipe, but never have I seen free water flow into a buried pipe, travel up hill, and emerge with force.

January 17, 2009
Super Bowl T-minus fourteen days
No running water means no flushing. We move to a hotel. A hotel with a bar. A bar that is out of Knob Creek. God hates me.

January 19, 2009
Super Bowl T-minus twelve days:
Plumber can't get a permit to repair the line until tomorrow because all city offices are closed due to Martin Luther King day. We become aware of CLUE. CLUE is a database maintained by insurance companies so that they can intimidate folks into not filing claims for water damage. If you file, you go in the CLUE database. When your insurance company drops you for filing the claim, you are not able to get homeowners insurance from anyone else.

Fortunately, it snows. We move out of the hotel to reduce the potential loss. We begin melting snow to flush. Flushing is a privilege not to be abused.

January 20, 2009

Super Bowl T-minus eleven days:

Got permit. Have to wait for the digging cops to mark the yard so we can dig. No idea when they will come. Apparently the digging corps are typical employees of the utilities. They may not show up till spring. We're still dehumidifying the basement. It's getting better.

January 21, 2009

Super Bowl T-minus ten days:

Some bastard painted lines on the snow in my yard. It's the gas guys. Now we're just waiting on the Middlesex Water Company. I am praying that the guy who paints the lines is more motivated and more competent than the guy who sends the bills out. They're not very good at billing people properly. Many tiles on the basement floor have come up. We remove them to allow the concrete to dry properly. Basement looks like hell, but we're making progress.

January 23, 2009

Super Bowl T-minus nine days:

The guy from Middlesex Water shows up and marks the line. Plumbers don't work on weekends. The basement floor is finally dry enough. We prime the floor, and put new tiles down. The carpets are cleaned, and the furniture is washed with Murphy's Oil Soap. We are getting there.

January 25, 2009
Super Bowl T-minus six days

It is four degrees outside. I have a good fire into the smoker. Two shoulders and eighteen slabs of loin back ribs. A couple of rough looking neighbors just happen by to see what's cooking. They are chronic Jets fans. Neither Steeler fans nor Ole Miss fans. I know why they are here. I show them my ax handle, they realize there is no barbecue for them, and they leave empty handed.

January 26, 2009
Super Bowl T-minus five days:
The Pagans Motorcycle club sends a plumber and a buttboy over at 7:00 am. A guy on a backhoe shows up moments later. By noon, we have water. Life is good.

January 27, 2009

Super Bowl T-minus four days:

Catfish is twelve years old. An email arrives from the Central Jersey Fireman's cook-off! They are having the contest this year. it will be on June 20, 2009. It just doesn't get any better than this. We can flush. The basement is ready for the Super Bowl, and we've received notice that our favorite barbecue contest, where we have done well, is back on!!! The very best thing about this barbecue contest is they have running water in the bathrooms.

I love running water.

February 1, 2009

Super Bowl Sunday

The Steelers beat the Cardinals 27-23 in Tampa.

The Worst Place Ever

Perhaps the worst job I ever had was at the same time the best job I ever had. I was working for a "call center" company. That's a nice way of saying "collections company." The place I worked was the third largest call center company in the world. It was run by a man who, with little room for doubt, was the world's biggest jerk. As CEO, he would host staff meetings in Manhattan that would start at 10 am, and run until 2:30 pm without a break… unless he needed to excuse himself for a moment. He had lunch brought in for himself, but no one else. He would pontificate as he picked at his baked chicken. He would put the phone on mute, and instruct someone at the table to ensure that the person speaking on the phone from one of our remote locations was fired by the end of the day. Everyone had a nickname. I was the Redneck. He was Voldemort.

For about half of my career at this place, I worked in New Jersey with a collection of lunatics. The Douchebag, my manager, was probably the finest manager I have ever worked for. Once, when I asked for direction on a matter, his reply was, "I don't care what you do, or how you do it. Just make the damn thing work." I may love this man.

His boss, Captain America, was incredibly effective at shielding us from the whims of Voldemort. The Big Wop was a giant Italian guy whose three-year-old girl regularly conveyed messages from the Big Wop's grandfather. Pretty cool, except that the Big Wop's grandfather had been dead for about twenty-five years. The Big Wop's grandfather trained horses when he was alive. He was pretty good at picking the horses. He, or perhaps the three-year-old girl, was still pretty good at picking horses even though he had been dead for a quarter century. The Greek was Don Rickles. One of the nicest guys you would ever meet, he had an uncanny ability to piss women off. Ben, the storage guy, was a chick magnet. Once, while at a strip joint in Atlantic City, a group of the strippers kidnapped Ben and it took him three days to escape. The Princess was the administrative assistant to Captain America. She was a former New Jersey women's prison guard who somehow became Captain America's admin during his time at Toys-R-Us. Her loyalty to Captain America was absolute. This whole damn circus used to work at Toys-R-Us. We had a couple of religious nuts in the mix. Both were members of competing cults, and used to argue frequently, each claiming the other was a "heretic." I used to enjoy setting them off until Douchebag told me I had to stop. This place was a madhouse. All of these guys were incredibly good at what they did, but they were all nuts too.

One day, The Douchebag came into the office. He walked over to the aisle where the Big Wop and The Greek sat. He looked down the aisle of cubicles and struck the pose of pitcher standing on the mound at a baseball game. The Big Wop was standing outside of The Greek's cubicle talking. The Douchebag went into a stretch and then threw a pretty good fastball, nailing the big Wop right on the kidney. The Big Wop hollered, and clutched his kidney. He glared at the Douchebag. "What the hell was that for?" he screamed, as if there might be a reasonable explanation for getting hit by a baseball in an office.

"Shut up, take your base," came the reply and the Douchebag walked off.

Nerf gun fights were a common occurrence. Everyone had the biggest, baddest Nerf gun they could buy stashed somewhere in their desk. I never saw what started Nerf gun battles, but when they occurred, whoever was paired with Captain America was sure to win. Captain America was probably the most gifted natural leader I ever met. He shouted commands to folks who he chose to be on his side, and God help you if you turned out to be on the other side. Death by Nerf gun isn't a pretty thing.

Suddenly, however, someone would shout, "India's down." The battle would stop. Someone else would shout, "I can see "Ickystan," or, "Manila is gone, too." You could hear loud tapping as keyboards were assaulted across the room. Shouts rang out as reports went back and forth, updating everyone as these raging lunatics checked their systems and ran diagnostics. In a matter of minutes, it was determined that an undersea cable somewhere had gone down. In a matter of minutes, our network traffic was rerouted over an alternate cable. Everyone shouted out their status as systems came back on line, and production returned to normal. This was the most incredible self-directing team I have ever seen.

When I first started there, we had an outage probably once a week. My systems were as flaky as any systems I have ever worked on. They were poorly configured, improperly maintained, unpatched, and unreliable. We were a 24/7 shop without a 24/7 infrastructure. Voldemort would absolutely not allow any maintenance outages. Most of the things that were wrong with our Unix boxes were big things, and fixes required, at the very minimum, a reboot to address. Just like nearly everyone else, I was getting flogged on a daily basis on the calls where we reviewed open issues. I had major systemic and fundamental problems that were regularly causing outages. They were not, however, going to get fixed without an outage, and I could not get an outage to fix them. It's a tough spot... but it was not without opportunity.

It dawned on me that all of the systems and network components were as poorly configured, improperly maintained, unpatched and unreliable as mine were. They too suffered outages on a routine basis. So, I staged fixes on my systems ready for the next opportunity. The next time we had an outage because of someone else's system I used the opportunity to implement a couple of fixes and I rebooted my environments. It took eight months to complete all of the remedial things. After those eight months of diligent and opportunistic work, my systems did not suffer another outage for twenty-four months. A full two years passed before a Unix box suffered a problem. By the time something failed, I had been found to be no longer necessary and had left.

It is true that no good deed goes unpunished. A mere six months after my servers became stable, my success brought me to the attention of Voldemort. Now, rather than working near the data center and enjoying a quiet liquid lunch at the Pub in the Hyatt on Rt. 10 in Parsippany, New Jersey, I was required to be in Manhattan at our corporate headquarters. Voldemort would hold meetings that would last for hours. No notes were ever taken, in fact it was strongly discouraged. At the conclusion of the meeting, there were no direct action items, no follow-ups planned, just a vague sense of being adrift on a sea of shifting requirements. Because we had so many people in the meeting, the meeting room could not seat everyone. Voldemort took to holding his meetings in a large walkway, a hall. He would sit and pontificate, and everyone else stood in the hall. These meetings would go on for hours. I attended exactly one.

After that one afternoon of standing in the hall on the 34th floor of the 334 Madison Ave, Manhattan, I was cured. I began to arrive at headquarters on Madison Ave early so that I had an opportunity check my environments and do any actual IT work that was necessary. My environments were clean and stable so usually there wasn't much to do. Then, I would make sure that Voldemort saw me. I would smile as I casually encountered him in a hallway. We would sometimes chat for moment about social stuff. Occasionally the furry little bastard would go on about his college days on the "sculling team" or perhaps about his amazing rhetorical triumphs in the debate club at Princeton. He was impressed that I studied at Oxford. Truth be told, he thought it was Oxford, England, and had he asked, I would have told him it was Oxford, Mississippi, home of Ole Miss. Hotty Toddy. After my brief encounter with Voldemort, I would then leave the office. We were on the 34th floor. I took the elevator down to the ground floor. I walked across 43rd street to a little Irish pub where I would watch soccer, eat lunch and drink wine until 4:00 pm. At that point, I returned to my office, collected my things, and began the trek home.

Just when you think it can't get any worse, it gets worse. When our Chief Technical Officer went out on medical leave Voldemort hired the Jolly Green Giant as our new senior executive fuzzy deluxe Vice President. He was about seven feet tall, and was consumed by a burning ambition to become CTO. He was, unfortunately, poorly equipped for his lofty goal, because despite having tremendous ambition, determination and drive, he was a putz with the intellect of a house mouse, the vision of a bat, and the leadership qualities of a three-legged, de-nutted beagle. I left on bad terms with him, as I don't suffer fools easily.

Between Voldemort and the Jolly Green Giant, the last year-and-a-half of my time there really sucked. It sucked more than any place I have ever been. But in that first year-and-a-half or two years there, I worked with the most incredible group of IT professionals I have ever seen assembled anywhere. All were crazy as outhouse rats but all worked together in a self-directing team that performed under amazingly adverse conditions and achieved a level of performance and raw competence that I have never seen matched anywhere... not at GE, not at Verizon, not at Merck, Bristol Myers Squibb, Sprint, or HP.

I have no doubt that I will never again work with a manager the caliber of the Douchebag, or a team like the one Captain America put together. At some point in your career, I hope you get to work with guys like them. They were definitely crazy, but damn they were good. I would do it all over again just to get to work with those guys.

A Good Kid

Several years ago, a kid about fifteen-years-old punched Catfish. The Fish was about eight at the time. As you would expect, I was not happy and I went to have a chat with the kid's parents. On asking one of the neighbors where the kid lived, I went there. When I found the house, the boy, his mother, and his grandparents were all in the backyard.

I've raised three kids and uncounted dogs. You develop an ability to 'read' a kid to some degree. I was watching this boy while I spoke with his mother and grandparents. Just from his posture, his demeanor, and the way he looked at me and his parents, I knew this boy had troubles, heavy troubles. He didn't have the eyes of a bad kid. He had the eyes of a kid who was just lost. Somewhere in the conversation with his mother and grandparents, I stopped being a pissed off dad, and I remembered the older kids while growing up in my neighborhood, Birdland.

I took the opportunity to tell this kid about one of the older kids in my neighborhood. This guy had no brothers or sisters, but he looked after the smaller kids in the neighborhood like they were his little brothers. He was the ultimate "you can do it" kind of guy. Despite my paralyzing fear of heights, he helped me find the courage to ride the zip line from a three-story tree house. He taught us all to play baseball, basketball and football. He showed me how to pole vault over a barbed wire fence using a bamboo pole he got from the carpet place. I can clearly remember this guy coaching me on how to sing Herman's Hermits songs with a proper English accent despite my thick southern drawl. My little brother perfected dribbling through his legs, spinning jump shots and trick dunks on this guy's dunk goal.

The kid listened to me as I told him about how this guy made us all better just by knowing him. To us, the smaller kids in Birdland, this guy was a superhero. The kid who punched Catfish just looked at me as I explained the impact this one kid had on the rest of us. I told him, "Be the kid that the little kids run to when they are in trouble. Don't be the kid they run from. Be the superhero."

I don't know what became of that kid. Fish never had any more trouble with him. After reflecting for a few minutes on growing up in Birdland, something struck me that I still contemplate to this very day. While I will never know what it's like to be a superhero, I do know what it's like to have known one.

Dining with History

Some are old men now, with gray hair. They are bent and broken, and have hearing aids. They walk with a little bit of a shuffle, or perhaps a cane or a limp, and some have hands that tremble a bit. A gaze into their eyes sometimes shows a hint of glaucoma. They are quiet, and mild, and courteous. They are gentle, and gentlemen, but once, long ago, they were fierce.

These are the men who crawled out of the sand at Normandy and freed Europe from the Nazis. They fought and died from island to island as they defeated Japan in the Pacific. They were the "Frozen Chosin" who fought their way out of a winter hell and rescued South Korea from the Communists. They fought in the jungles of Vietnam and the streets Saigon to the mountains of Cambodia. The fought on the beaches of Grenada and in the streets of Panama. From the shifting desert sands in Iraq to the rugged expanse of Afghanistan they carried rucksacks and guns. They went in harm's way and lived, and have never forgotten their friends who died.

Yesterday, we fed them barbecue at the Clark American Legion.

Living in an age when football players who kneel are mistaken for heroes, it was an honor to dine with so many real ones.

Attacked by a Mad Dog

I am distraught.

My chocolate lab, Dixie, whom we have raised from a pup, came to me this morning and informed me that I had offended her and that due to the racist connotations of her name, she will no longer answer to that name, preferring to be addressed as "Svatchime."

"What? Offended? How can you be offended? You're a dog!" I asked as I scratched her behind her ear.

"Someone told me that I was named after a horrible racist song that glorifies slavery and oppression and that I have always been horribly oppressed my entire life by you, you hateful bigot," she growled.

"Who told you that? Was it Isadore?" I asked as I offered her a piece of bacon. Isadore is a mean little terrier/poodle mix who lives behind us. She doesn't like me and barks a lot.

Dixie nodded as she devoured the bacon, and paused just for a second to ask, "What's a song?"

Of course, I was shocked, and not just because my dog was speaking with me, or because she was offended by her own name, but also because of her new name. "Svatchime" is what conservative radio host Bud Grant used to call Mario Cuomo when he was governor of New York… it's Italian for "the impotent one."

Do you know what "Svatchime" means?" I asked.

"No, but I like it and Isador says that it can mean whatever I want it to mean," came the reply.

While trying to wrap my brain around all this, I heard a loud ruckus erupt outside the house. I looked out the window, and a small but loud band of feral cats were in the front yard singing 'Dixie' while waving dead mice and Confederate flags.

"Who are they?" I asked.

"They are your confederates, you hateful bigot. Can I have some more bacon?" came the reply.

"No more bacon for you. Why are they here?"

"Isadore invited them," Dixie replied. "She said that you racists should hang out together. I really want some more bacon, you fascist pig."

"They are feral cats, you stupid dog, and I'm not a racist! No bacon for you," I reminded her.

"You're a mean spirited, greedy, white supremacist sexist, xenophobic homophile, and a racist, Zionist, anti-Semite pig! I want more bacon! Look at your friends and look what you named me, you race baiting skunk!" said Dixie in anger.

Using my Airsoft rifle, I persuaded each cat to leave.

Dixie was angry, but now I was too. I pointed my Airsoft gun at Dixie and said softly, "They are not my friends, Dixie is your name, and…"

"SQUIRREL!" Dixie screamed as she leaped at the sliding glass door and began to bark madly.

It isn't necessarily insane to talk to a dog, but trying to reason with one might be.

www.ingramcontent.com/pod-product-compliance
Lightning Source LLC
Chambersburg PA
CBHW070424010526
44118CB00014B/1899